AMANTI & IMANI SLAM DUNK LAZY TALK MINI DICTIONARY:

WHO'S YO AUTHOR?

HACIMA AMANTI LISAYA-KELLEY

iUniverse®

AMANTI & IMANI SLAM DUNK LAZY TALK MINI DICTIONARY: WHO'S YO AUTHOR?

iUniverse books may be ordered through booksellers or by contacting:

iUniverse
1663 Liberty Drive
Bloomington, IN 47403
www.iuniverse.com
1-800-Authors (1-800-288-4677)

ISBN: 978-1-5320-7809-5 (sc)
ISBN: 978-1-5320-7810-1 (e)

Print information available on the last page.

iUniverse rev. date: 07/12/2019

GIVE CREDITS TO

Lakia Turner-Davis

Kason A.L.L. Davis

Justice Kason-Levar Staples

Akiam Imani Justice K. Staples

Kareem Levar-Huggins Staples

CONTENTS

REASONS FOR CREATING THIS TYPE OF DICTIONARY

There are lots of ways to pronounce each word in a dictionary, such as: Slang and Ghetto Talk. Well from my experience in life growing up to be in my late 30's now, I call it Lazy Talk. And I call it "Lazy Talk", since I know how to properly pronounce each word. I'm just lazy and pronounce it the way I feel like it – which is to me "Lazy Talk".

A lot of people know it as Slang or Ghetto Talk but everyone in each community, each city, each state, each country has a different type of way to properly say a word and/or say it in a way that isn't "Properly" spoken out as a dictionary would have it. So, it is "Lazy Talk" to me, since people look at "Slang/Ghetto Talk" like only a specific type of people would call it Slang or Ghetto Talk But Lazy Talk can easily be said and written in each community, each city, each state and each country.

As any dictionary, you will have a word printed, pronounced, and defined as Lazy Talk. Then the proper talk word, pronunciation, and definition – under the Lazy Talk word, pronunciation, and definition.

(A)

Lazy Talk Word:
Abbrevate – a shorter version of any word.
Proper Talk Word:
Abbreviate – a smaller word abbreviated or shortened.

Lazy Talk Word:
Abdamin – lower area of the stomach.
Proper Talk Word:
Abdomen – the part of the body between the navel and genital area.

Lazy Talk Word:
And Bet – cool points in a conversation.
Proper Talk Word:
Abet – to encourage or to have incite.

Lazy Talk Word:
Abilatey – the act of being able to do something.
Proper Talk Word:
Ability – a talent from intelligence.

Lazy Talk Word:
'Bout – the first or second that you do or say something.
Proper Talk Word:
About – approximately.

Lazy Talk Word:
Buv' – the up top of something; to be better.
Proper Talk Word:
Above – overhead; higher place or rank.

Lazy Talk Word:
Aboose – treatment an animal or human that is considered to not be fairly right physically and/or mentally.
Proper Talk Word:
Abuse – the bad treatment of a person, place, or thing.

Lazy Talk Word:
A'sent – not present.
Proper Talk Word:
Absent – staying away by choice or not by choice.

Lazy Talk Word:
A mind is gone – to be through with; not factually right.
Proper Talk Word:
Absent minded – forgetful and preoccupied.

Lazy Talk Word:
Asolv – to verify if someone is truthful or a liar.
Proper Talk Word:
Absolve – to clear of blame or guilt.

Lazy Talk Word:
Asorv – to take something in and it is built up; to retrieve something.
Proper Talk Word:
Absorb – To take in or soak in or up.

Lazy Talk Word:
Asurd – difficult with being factually reasonable.
Proper Talk Word:
Absurd – ridiculous and unreasonable.

Lazy Talk Word:
Absalootly – to be sure or positive about something or someone.
Proper Talk Word:
Absolutely – perfectly complete; to be positive.

Lazy Talk Word:
Astanence – to stop doing something.
Proper Talk Word:
Abstinence – refrain from or stop from drinking of food.

Lazy Talk Word:
Akcent – a foreign language mixed with the American language that sounds slightly different – depending on what state and/or country the person is from or resided in.
Proper Talk Word:
Accent – to pronounce a word characteristically; (Note: see character proper talk).

Lazy Talk Word:
'Complish – to be rewarded with something.
Proper Talk Word:
Accomplish – to succeed in doing something.

Lazy Talk Word:
'Commadate – to give a favor to someone or something.
Proper Talk Word:
Accommodate – to supply with or give a favor.

Lazy Talk Word:
Acoun – bank statement or any other statement; a membership to something or someone.
Proper Talk Word:
Account – an explanation or report.

Lazy Talk Word:
Acoomyoulate – to absorb something or someone.
Proper Talk Word:
Accumulate – to mount up to someone or something.

Lazy Talk Word:
Acrit – to fit to a "T"; to be right presented by all facts and no opinions.
Proper Talk Word:
Accurate – to be correct, exact, and no errors.

Lazy Talk Word:
Cuesing – to put blame on someone or something.
Proper Talk Word:
Accusing – to blame someone for something or someone for false errors.

Lazy Talk Word:
'Cusom – to be used to or familiar with something physically or orally.
Proper Talk Word:
Accustom – to be familiarized.

Lazy Talk Word:
Ake – to be in pain physically.
Proper Talk Word:
Ache – a dull, steady pain.

Lazy Talk Word:
'Noledge – to be aware of someone or something; to be intelligent.
Proper Talk Word:
Acknowledge – to admit the existence or truth of.

Lazy Talk Word:
Aqwire – to have someone or something in your possession.
Proper Talk Word:
Acquire – to gain possession of.

Lazy Talk Word:
'quitted – charge to be dismissed.
Proper Talk Word:
Acquitted – to clear someone or something of a charge.

Lazy Talk Word:
Actwall – to be a fact not an opinion about anything.
Proper Talk Word:
Actual – in existence or to be real.

Lazy Talk Word:
Adap – to adjust or get used to something or someone.
Proper Talk Word:
Adapt – to adjust to new or different conditions.

Lazy Talk Word:
Addick – someone who abused drugs or anything else.
Proper Talk Word:
Addict – a person that's hooked on narcotics.

Lazy Talk Word:
Adres – a street name with city, state, & zip code; talk to.
Proper Talk Word:
Address – to speak to; or the location of an organization or person.

Lazy Talk Word:
Depted – very smart and intelligent.
Proper Talk Word:
Adept – highly skilled.

Lazy Talk Word:
Adakwit – the right amount of something needed.
Proper Talk Word:
Adequate – able to satisfy a requirement.

Lazy Talk Word:
Adew – farewell.
Proper Talk Word:
Adieu – farewell.

Lazy Talk Word:
Ajus' – to get use to anything (person, place, or thing).
Proper Talk Word:
Adjust – to regulate or adapt to something and someone.

Lazy Talk Word:
Amenister – something being given to someone.
Proper Talk Word:
Administer – to manage.

Lazy Talk Word:
Amiyer – to praise to someone or something that has been accomplished positively.

Proper Talk Word:
Admire – to have esteem and respect.

Lazy Talk Word:
Adrinalen – the point of hyperactive in the body.
Proper Talk Word:
Adrenaline – Epinephrine.

Lazy Talk Word:
Adriff – don't have the right type of direction.
Proper Talk Word:
Adrift – floating.

Lazy Talk Word:
Avans – to be at your high peak in anything.
Proper Talk Word:
Advance – to move forward; or to progress in anything.

Lazy Talk Word:
Afta – next in order of anything.
Proper Talk Word:
After – later; behind; in pursuit of.

Lazy Talk Word:
Afta Maf – after something happen; the result of something.
Proper Talk Word:
Aftermath – a consequence from doing something.

Lazy Talk Word:
Afta shoque – how someone or something feels after something happens.
Proper Talk Word:
Aftershock – a quake of lesser magnitude that follows a large earthquake in the same area.

Lazy Talk Word:
Afta word – when something happens in the 2nd place.
Proper Talk Word:
Afterward – in or at a later time.

Lazy Talk Word:
Agann – doing anything more than one time.
Proper Talk Word:
Again – once more.

Lazy Talk Word:
Agence – to be the opposite side of someone or something.
Proper Talk Word:
Against – in a direction or course opposite to.

Lazy Talk Word:
Aje – how old you are; anything that grows old.
Proper Talk Word:
Age – the length of time someone or something has existed.

Lazy Talk Word:
Ayegencie – a business and/ or company.
Proper Talk Word:
Agency – operation; a business or service acting for others.

Lazy Talk Word:
Ha Ha Ha – laughing moment.
Proper Talk Word:
Aha – laughing moment.

Lazy Talk Word:
Ahid – to be in front of someone or something; to be #1 instead of #2.
Proper Talk Word:
Ahead – at the front or in advance.

Lazy Talk Word:
Aight – ok; understandable; down for whatever.
Proper Talk Word:
Alright – confirmation of what is being done physically or said orally; to agree as to understand the information, etc.

Lazy Talk Word:
Ame – to position yourself perfectly or near perfect.
Proper Talk Word:
Aim – the direction of something positioned; intentions.

Lazy Talk Word:
Ain – to be surprised; can't believe it; to not have.

Proper Talk Word:
Ain't - contraction of "am not", "is not", "has not", and "have not".

Lazy Talk Word:
Ain dat' a bitch – can't believe what you saw, heard or did.
Proper Talk Word:
Ain't that a bitch – what someone did was not been approved of.

Lazy Talk Word:
Ayer Condisna – the control of the air being cold or hot.
Proper Talk Word:
Air Conditioner – to control or lower the temperature and humidity.

Lazy Talk Word:
Ille – the walk way in an auditorium or such, etc.
Proper Talk Word:
Aisle – a passage way between rows of seats.

Lazy Talk Word:
Alkimy – refer to science the early primary change

of gold and/or silver with metal.

Proper Talk Word:
Alchemy – an early kind of chemistry concerned primarily with changing common metals into gold.

Lazy Talk Word:
Alcoehall - used to rub on skin for sanitation before receiving a needle puncture; a beverage that has liquor on it.

Proper Talk Word:
Alcohol – an intoxicating liquor; or rubbing alcohol pads or bottle.

Lazy Talk Word:
Aldamen – membership with the political legislative office.

Proper Talk Word:
Alderman – a member of a municipal legislative body.

Lazy Talk Word:
Algibra – mathematical problems in the form of equations and fractions.

Proper Talk Word:
Algebra – a form of mathematics dealing with symbols and equations, etc.

Lazy Talk Word:
Aleus – a name that may or may not be legal.

Proper Talk Word:
Alias – an assumed named.

Lazy Talk Word:
Aline – to form two things together that are parallel – whether an oral conversation or physical action.

Proper Talk Word:
Align – to arrange in a line; take sides with one person in a 2-way conversation that can be professional and/or personal.

Lazy Talk Word:
Alamoenie – money received with a divorce settlement.

Proper Talk Word:
Alimony – an allowance for support paid to a former spouse.

Lazy Talk Word:
Alyve – to have a soul and life.
Proper Talk Word:
Alive – having life; in operation; active; and living.

Lazy Talk Word:
Alkilay – the chemistry of a person, place, or thing.
Proper Talk Word:
Alkali – in chemistry; a base.

Lazy Talk Word:
Alayge – saying something or doing something that may or may not be a fact; may have solved a problem; allegedly may have done something or not within reality.
Proper Talk Word:
Allege – to assert without proof.

Lazy Talk Word:
Aleegence – to have loyalty to a person, place or thing.
Proper Talk Word:
Allegiance – loyalty to a nation, sovereign, or cause.

Lazy Talk Word:
All Goodness – "oh my", "oh goodness"; something must about to happen.
Proper Talk Word:
All God – "oh my"; "oh lord"; ruler of the world.

Lazy Talk Word:
Allagata – a large ground or water animal that is teeth to bite and kill a human; wild animal.
Proper Talk Word:
Alligator – a large reptile with a shorter snout than the related crocodiles.

Lazy Talk Word:
Alytarashun – the same sound and syllables in a word.
Proper Talk Word:
Alliteration – the occurrence of two or more words having the same initial sound.

Lazy Talk Word:
Alouw – to be approved by someone to do anything.

Proper Talk Word:
Allow – to let happen; to acknowledge or admit.

Lazy Talk Word:
Ahminac – a book that consists of weather forecast.

Proper Talk Word:
Almanac – a calendar with weather forecasts and other useful information.

Lazy Talk Word:
Aulmz – helping low income by giving money or food.

Proper Talk Word:
Alms – money or goods given to the poor.

Lazy Talk Word:
Alfabet – all English letters in order from A thru Z.

Proper Talk Word:
Alphabet – the letters of a language, arranged in a fixed order.

Lazy Talk Word:
Allpiene – to refer to a mountain.

Proper Talk Word:
Alpine – relating to high mountains.

Lazy Talk Word:
Alreddy – did something at a prior time; previously.

Proper Talk Word:
Already – by this time.

Lazy Talk Word:
Altinit – plan b or second option.

Proper Talk Word:
Alternate – to go back and forth; following in order sequentially.

Lazy Talk Word:
Altow – low pitch voice sound when singing.

Proper Talk Word:
Alto – a low female singing voice.

Lazy Talk Word:
Aloomna -a college graduate; high school graduate.

Proper Talk Word:
Alumna – graduate of
a school, college, or
university.

Lazy Talk Word:
All ways – to do something
at all time.
Proper Talk Word:
Always – to be continuously
in anything.

Lazy Talk Word:
Ambishun – very bold
attitude of being a good
achiever by reaching a goal
that you set.
Proper Talk Word:
Ambition – a strong desire
to achieve something; the
will to succeed; a goal.

Lazy Talk Word:
Aman – the word used
biblically to show you finish
a prayer; thank goodness
it's complete; the end; the
author of this book root
name, which is the middle
name.

Proper Talk Word:
Amen – so be it; the word
used by Jesus Christ when
finishing the Lord's Prayer.

Lazy Talk Word:
Amin – to teach what is
right professionally and
personally.
Proper Talk Word:
Amend – to improve; to
correct.

Lazy Talk Word:
Amenatie – social
courtesies.
Proper Talk Word:
Amenity – a comfort or
convenience.

Lazy Talk Word:
Ameable – a person of a
good heart; Godly natured.
Proper Talk Word:
Amiable – good natured;
friendly.

Lazy Talk Word:
Amneesa – to forget.
Proper Talk Word:
Amnesia – loss of memory.

Lazy Talk Word:
Amonte – the value of anything.
Proper Talk Word:
Amount – a total or sum; to reach as a total.

Lazy Talk Word:
Amplaphie – increase or bigger than anything.
Proper Talk Word:
Amplify – to enlarge, extend, or increase. To make louder.

Lazy Talk Word:
Amoose – to entertain.
Proper Talk Word:
Amuse – divert.

Lazy Talk Word:
Analasis – to give a detailed type of report; to verify.
Proper Talk Word:
Analysis – the separation of a whole into its parts for study and interpretation.

Lazy Talk Word:
Anatomie – the cell of an organism.

Proper Talk Word:
Anatomy – the science of the structure of organisms.

Lazy Talk Word:
Andsesder – avoid family member from a family tree.
Proper Talk Word:
Ancestor – a person from whom another has descended.

Lazy Talk Word:
Anksent – old things, such as: person, place or thing.
Proper Talk Word:
Ancient – belonging to times long past.

Lazy Talk Word:
Anah – yes or ahhh.
Proper Talk Word:
And a – yes and a; I got it.

Lazy Talk Word:
An' what – and what; now what; cissed up.
Proper Talk Word:
And What – and now what's next, what's happening.

Lazy Talk Word:
Andnadote – a little comedy moment.
Proper Talk Word:
Anecdote – a short account of an interesting or humorous incident.

Lazy Talk Word:
Angle – a kind and loving individual.
Proper Talk Word:
Angel – one of the immortal beings to which is an attendant upon God.

Lazy Talk Word:
Anga – to have a mad attitude towards someone or something.
Proper Talk Word:
Anger – to make or become angry.

Lazy Talk Word:
Angal – a algebra symbol that is formed with tow lines, which can be in many forms.

Proper Talk Word:
Angle – the figure formed by two lines diverging from a common point.

Lazy Talk Word:
Angwish – great physical or mental pain.
Proper Talk Word:
Anguish – to torment.

Lazy Talk Word:
Annamul – a beast or an attitude out of control.
Proper Talk Word:
Animal – an organism distinguished from a plant by such characteristics as the ability to move; sensual physical as distinguished from spiritual.

Lazy Talk Word:
Anemate – a cartoon character.
Proper Talk Word:
Animate – to give life to; to make a pretend character alive.

Lazy Talk Word:
Ancle – the area of the body connected between foot and calf muscle – which is the bottom part of the leg.
Proper Talk Word:
Ankle – the joint that connects the foot with the leg.

Lazy Talk Word:
Annowse – to say a speech in front of a large crowd or audience.
Proper Talk Word:
Announce – to bring to public notice.

Lazy Talk Word:
Anoie – to be a nag or get on someone's nerves.
Proper Talk Word:
Annoy – to bother or irritate.

Lazy Talk Word:
Annuwal – a year of anything.
Proper Talk Word:
Annual – a yearly episode.

Lazy Talk Word:
Annol – to have a married be over-with like it never happened.
Proper Talk Word:
Annul – to nullify or cancel a marriage.

Lazy Talk Word:
Anonamus – to be hidden from everyone or a specific person.
Proper Talk Word:
Anonymous – having an unknown or withheld person, place, or thing.

Lazy Talk Word:
Anuva – a second of anything; more than one.
Proper Talk Word:
Another – additional; one more.

Lazy Talk Word:
Ansir – the reply to anything; to respond to.
Proper Talk Word:
Answer – a solution or result; to serve a purpose.

Lazy Talk Word:
Antisapate – to realize beforehand; to look forward to.
Proper Talk Word:
Anticipate – foresee; to prevent or forestall.

Lazy Talk Word:
Andteek – old fashion ornaments or houseware.
Proper Talk Word:
Antique – belonging to an earlier period; an object having special value because of its' age.

Lazy Talk Word:
Anyplase – to be in a building or outside of a building anywhere.
Proper Talk Word:
Anyplace – to; in; or at anywhere.

Lazy Talk Word:
Apartman – a place of your own with one to 3 bedrooms in a building with other tenants living there as well.

Proper Talk Word:
Apartment – a room or suite of rooms for dwelling.

Lazy Talk Word:
Apecks – the highest peak of anything.
Proper Talk Word:
Apex – the highest point of something.

Lazy Talk Word:
Aplum – to have self-confidence.
Proper Talk Word:
Aplomb – to be poise.

Lazy Talk Word:
AreKaid – a room full of different games to play.
Proper Talk Word:
Arcade – an amusement center with coin-operated electronic and video games.

Lazy Talk Word:
Areena – place where a play or skit is performed.
Proper Talk Word:
Arena – the area in the center of an amphitheater or

stadium where contests are held.

Lazy Talk Word:
Ass – I can't believe that; a buttocks.
Proper Talk Word:
As - used in comparisons to refer to the extent or degree of something.

Lazy Talk Word:
Ascqe – to find out something through questions.
Proper Talk Word:
Ask – to put question to; to inquire about.

Lazy Talk Word:
Ass Fucking Whole – a belligerent or loud spoken person.
Proper Talk Word:
Asswhole – the butt of a person or animal.

Lazy Talk Word:
Attum – a science element.
Proper Talk Word:
Atom – the smallest unit of a chemical element.

Lazy Talk Word:
Arthur – a original preparer or signed published writer.
Proper Talk Word:
Author – a writer; an originator or creator.

Lazy Talk Word:
Ayevow – to acknowledge openly
Proper Talk Word:
Avow – to confess.

Lazy Talk Word:
Awored – a prize; a grant for high performance or quality.
Proper Talk Word:
Award – a decision to give someone a prize for advanced performance.

(B)

Lazy Talk Word:
Babe – a new born child or a figure of speech when in a relationship.
Proper Talk Word:
Baby – an infant; cuddle.

Lazy Talk Word:
Bay Bay – a popular way of saying baby; a newborn child; love nickname for a couple.
Proper Talk Word:
Baby – an infant; to pamper, cuddle.

Lazy Talk Word:
Bachla – a single male/female that have a potential to have several people that are interested in them; a degree that comes directly after the Associates.
Proper Talk Word:
Bachelor – an unmarried man or woman; An undergraduate degree.

Lazy Talk Word:
Baquebone – your spine in your back; or a person saying – I got you.
Proper Talk Word:
Backbone – the vertebrate spine; a main support; strength of character.

Lazy Talk Word:
[I be] Back – leaving and will return.
Proper Talk Word:
[I'll be] Back soon – will arrive soon in the future "of hours instead of days or months".

Lazy Talk Word:
Bad Ass – someone with a popular attitude.
Proper Talk Word:
Bad as – not good; regretful.

Lazy Talk Word:
Bae Bae – a newborn baby; cool points for a person that's beautiful and/or young.
Proper Talk Word:
Baby – an infant; a name given by a significant other.

Lazy Talk Word:
Bagidge – suitcase; someone having something left that is old.
Proper Talk Word:
Baggage – luggage.

Lazy Talk Word:
Bail/Baila – to be released from a commitment; a persons' name.
Proper Talk Word:
Bail/Bale – money supplied as a guarantee that an arrested person will appear for trial.

Lazy Talk Word:
Bannen – to prevent someone or something doing something.
Proper Talk Word:
Banning – a persons' name; when someone stops the action of someone or something.

Lazy Talk Word:
Banque – a place of business that issues and receives cash money, money orders, certified checks, and cd's.
Proper Talk Word:
Bank – an establishment for safekeeping, handling, and lending money; to have confidence in.

Lazy Talk Word:
Barbique – the type of sauce used for different meats at a family/friend gathering or cookout.
Proper Talk Word:
Bar-be-cue – a grill or outdoor fireplace for roasting meat; to cook meat overtop coal while coal is in a cooking grill.

Lazy Talk Word:
Barericks – the military for e-4 bedrooms in a military barracks building; barracks bedroom.
Proper Talk Word:
Barracks – a building used to hold soldiers; a presidents' name.

Lazy Talk Word:
Basqet Bawl – a specific type of ball used for sports; to throw to someone or in a net; throw a ball; to play a sport with it.
Proper Talk Word:
Basket Ball – a game in which players try to throw

a large ball through an elevated hoop.

Lazy Talk Word:
Beech Bum – a person that dress bummy while living at a beach.
Proper Talk Word:
Beach Bum – a person that is dressed non-professional at a sandy shore.

Lazy Talk Word:
Beest – an animal; a title or name; a military motto.
Proper Talk Word:
Beast – an animal.

Lazy Talk Word:
Bid – a place to lay down and relax/sleep; to place a bet on something.
Proper Talk Word:
Bed – a piece of furniture for sleeping; to put in bed.

Lazy Talk Word:
Bafow – to go first to someone else.
Proper Talk Word:
Before – to let someone go ahead of you.

Lazy Talk Word:
Baleave – to agree; to accept a factual statement; to believe in God.
Proper Talk Word:
Believe – to accept as true or real; to support; to believe in Jesus Christ.

Lazy Talk Word:
Baligarant – a hostile person; ugly attitude to the extreme of being upset; loud and ignorant.
Proper Talk Word:
Belligerent – agressively hostile; waging war.

Lazy Talk Word:
Bybal – a Godly book that is written from Gods word directly through a prophet.
Proper Talk Word:
Bible – the sacred book of christianity; the scriptures, the sacred book of judaism.

Lazy Talk Word:
Big Staples – a person's name; to be the boss.

Proper Talk Word:
[A] Big Staple – to have large staples for a stapler.

Lazy Talk Word:
Bich – a non-formal way to approach someone with conversation.
Proper Talk Word:
Bitch – a female dog; profanity.

Lazy Talk Word:
Bloo Lawe – sunday activities regulations and law.
Proper Talk Word:
Blue Law – a law that controls the activities of a church environment.
Lazy Talk Word:
Bloo Print – a diagram on paper completed by an engineer of a town, city, and/or state; blueprint to build a fence around a house, etc.
Proper Talk Word:
Blue Print – a detailed plan, as of an architectural design.

Lazy Talk Word:
Bootay – a popular way of saying booty or Phat Butt.
Proper Talk Word:
Booty – a private part.

Lazy Talk Word:
Bottum Lign – the main point; the big picture.
Proper Talk Word:
Bottom Line – the lowest line on a financial statement, showing net loss or gain; a final answer.

Lazy Talk Word:
Breefcayse – a hand held leather box shaped case that is used to transport important things in it.
Proper Talk Word:
Briefcase – a small bag that is square or rectangle shaped that is used to hold documents or materials in it; Mostly used for work or court.

Lazy Talk Word:
Brem – a projecting edge of a hat.

Proper Talk Word:
Brim – the uppermost edge of a cup.

Lazy Talk Word:
Brotha – a person you close with as friends that begin to feel as though they are your brother; a family member born by the same mother and/or father; or by marriage.

Proper Talk Word:
Brother – a male having the same parents as another; one who has a close bond with another; a family member.

Lazy Talk Word:
Bucq – to get pumped up; to make intimidated.

Proper Talk Word:
Buck – a name brand for a men's sweatsuit; to someone scared or to have an obnoxious attitude or appearance.

Lazy Talk Word:
Bucq Wyld – someone popular raising interest to common people they know; to be advanced in something.

Proper Talk Word:
Buck Wild – to have energy to compete with someone or something.

Lazy Talk Word:
By By – a saying from a leap frog toy; too leave someone; a gesture.

Proper Talk Word:
Bye Bye – used to express farewell.

(C)

Lazy Talk Word:
Cashay – a hiding spot for cash or money.

Proper Talk Word:
Cachet – a seal on a document; a mark of quality or distinction.

Lazy Talk Word:
Kaddy – a person's name; a car's nickname.

Proper Talk Word:
Caddy – a movie name;
to drive a caddy or a
Cadillac car.

Lazy Talk Word:
Cadebt – a military officer
title; a police department
title; a JROTC training
title.
Proper Talk Word:
Cadet – a student training
to be a military officer, or
a police cadet, or a JROTC
trainee graduate.

Lazy Talk Word:
Cain – can't do something;
a person's name.
Proper Talk Word:
Can't – to prohibit from
doing something.

Lazy Talk Word:
Kanyun – a skinny area
with cliff walls that run
deep; a place in a mountain
with flat surfaced.
Proper Talk Word:
Canyon – a narrow valley
with steep cliff walls.

Lazy Talk Word:
Kapeable – being able
to understand; to be
competent.
Proper Talk Word:
Capable – something that
is done properly; can do
something.

Lazy Talk Word:
Kash – money to spend on
anything.
Proper Talk Word:
Cash – ready money; to
exchange for money.

Lazy Talk Word:
Seemeant – a construction
material used to create and/
or maintain for driving on
top of; the street.
Proper Talk Word:
Cement – a construction
material made of powdered
rock, clay, and water that
hardens after pouring; any
adhesive, glue; someone's
name.

Lazy Talk Word:
Sirtafy – to be able to say that you are a guarantee to get a certificate or a job, etc.
Proper Talk Word:
Certify – to confirm formally as true; to guarantee.

Lazy Talk Word:
Challinge – to have a contest; test ability.
Proper Talk Word:
Challenge – a call to engage in a contest; a demand for an explanation or identification.

Lazy Talk Word:
Champeun – to have first place in a competition or game.
Proper Talk Word:
Champion – one that holds first place; an advocate; to fight for; support.

Lazy Talk Word:
Chanze – an opportunity.

Proper Talk Word:
Chance – luck; fate; probability; an opportunity; a risk.

Lazy Talk Word:
Chank – to sing a melody.
Proper Talk Word:
Chant – a melody in which a number of words are sung on each note; a monotonous voice; to sing.

Lazy Talk Word:
Kayos – drama; hostility.
Proper Talk Word:
Chaos – total disorder.

Lazy Talk Word:
Showfer – a escort limo service driver.
Proper Talk Word:
Chauffeur – one employed to drive a private automobile.

Lazy Talk Word:
Chairish – to put on a pedestal.
Proper Talk Word:
Cherish – to hold dearly.

Lazy Talk Word:
Chest – a persons' top part of their torso; a game for 2 players.
Proper Talk Word:
Chess – a board game for 2 players.

Lazy Talk Word:
Kwier – a chorus with in a church, school, or college.
Proper Talk Word:
Choir – a group of singers; a repeated refrain; to sing or to utter together.

Lazy Talk Word:
Clairafie – to become understandable or comprehensive.
Proper Talk Word:
Clarify – to make or become clear.

Lazy Talk Word:
Clamint – merciful; a persons' name.
Proper Talk Word:
Clement – merciful; mild, as the weather.

Lazy Talk Word:
Klimax – the highest point of excitement; to have an orgasm.
Proper Talk Word:
Climax – the point of greatest intensity or excitement; to sexually cum (or an orgasm).

Lazy Talk Word:
Kollig – a school designed to be at a more advanced level than high school.
Proper Talk Word:
College – a school or a higher learning.

Lazy Talk Word:
Cum on – to go ahead; to go forward; orgasm.
Proper Talk Word:
Come on – to be a leader, leading followers.

Lazy Talk Word:
Commin – that's messed up.
Proper Talk Word:
Common – to be in the familiar area or right factual conversation, etc.

Lazy Talk Word:
Kontint – to satisfy without doubting.
Proper Talk Word:
Content – that which is contained in something; substance; satisfaction.

Lazy Talk Word:
Coppy write – to copy someone writings or to make a duplex copy.
Proper Talk Word:
Copyright – to publish something that was created by an official author.

Lazy Talk Word:
Coodin – can't do something.
Proper Talk Word:
Couldn't – to prohibit from doing something.

Lazy Talk Word:
Countsil – to evaluate and give advice to.
Proper Talk Word:
Counsel – advice or guidance; lawyer or group of lawyers; to advise. a doctor that gives medical advice for a mental or injury health diagnosis.

Lazy Talk Word:
Coreridge – to be brave.
Proper Talk Word:
Courage – resistance to fear; bravery.

Lazy Talk Word:
Creait – to be the original and first to do something.
Proper Talk Word:
Create – to cause to exist; originate.

(D)

Lazy Talk Word:
Dang it – OMG; can't stop something from happening.
Proper Talk Word:
Daggit – OMG; didn't mean to do something; mistake.

Lazy Talk Word:
Dag – a little upset cause something happened.
Proper Talk Word:
Dang – to cause to dangle.

Lazy Talk Word:
Dame – a water way.
Proper Talk Word:
Dam – to construct a
waterway across the river; to
obstruct.

Lazy Talk Word:
Damm – to condemn; dog
on it; shucks; a piece of land
filled with water.
Proper Talk Word:
Damn – to be upset; a
waterway; curse word
(profanity); a river, lake
and/or pond.

Lazy Talk Word:
Dannse – to move your
body in a rhythm from or
while listening to music.
Proper Talk Word:
Dance – to move
rhythmically to music;
series of rhythmical motions
and steps; a gather or piece
of music for dancing.

Lazy Talk Word:
Dapp – to give a fancy or
popular hand shake; to
show appreciation.

Proper Talk Word:
Dap – neatly dressed;
stylish; small and active
with hand shake or body
gesture(s); letting the fly
bob lightly on the water
without letting the line
touch the water.

Lazy Talk Word:
Daite – to go out with your
significant other to a public
place or building for to be
romantic; the calendar with
day, year, and month.
Proper Talk Word:
Date – the time at which
something happens; the
day of the month; an
appointment to meet
socially; to originate;
to make or have social
engagements with.

Lazy Talk Word:
Debbet Kard – card used
to receive cash from a bank
atm machine.
Proper Talk Word:
Debit Card – a backcard
with which purchases are

charged directly to a bank account.

Lazy Talk Word:
Dedakate – to devote to.
Proper Talk Word:
Dedicate – to set apart for special purposes; to inscribe.

Lazy Talk Word:
Depe – to be fully profound.
Proper Talk Word:
Deep – in depth; extending far down, back, or inward. Learned; profound; extreme.

Lazy Talk Word:
Delivearit – to be careful when making decisions.
Proper Talk Word:
Deliberate – to consider carefully; intentional; careful deciding; unhurried.

Lazy Talk Word:
Daliscous – something of good taste.
Proper Talk Word:
Delicious – highly pleasing to the taste.

Lazy Talk Word:
Dinomanation – something of good taste.
Proper Talk Word:
Denomination – a name; a unit in a system of currency or weights; a religious group or sect.

Lazy Talk Word:
Denewmen – the solution of a plot of a play or novel.
Proper Talk Word:
De'nouement – the outcome of a series of events.

Lazy Talk Word:
Discize – to modify the appearance of to prevent the real and original recognition.
Proper Talk Word:
Disguise – the condition of being disguised; something that serves as disguise.

Lazy Talk Word:
Doc – the area by the water in the ocean that has enlarged rocks for people to sit on to enjoy the view.

Proper Talk Word:
Dock – to clip or cut off; to withhold a part of salary.

Lazy Talk Word:
Dowg – an animal that barks, protects you, and can be used in a dog fight.

Proper Talk Word:
Dog – a domesticated mammal related to wolves and foxes.

Lazy Talk Word:
Dogonit – didn't mean to.

Proper Talk Word:
Dog on it – to not have control of a situation; darn.

Lazy Talk Word:
Domanaite – to control or rule.

Proper Talk Word:
Dominate – to be most prominent among; to overlook from a height; to be a dominat in the bed room sexually or at work as a professional boss.

Lazy Talk Word:
Doe – money; bread.

Proper Talk Word:
Dough – a mixture of flour and other ingredients baked as bread, pastry, etc.; cash.

(E)

Lazy Talk Word:
Erne – to work for an accomplishment.

Proper Talk Word:
Earn – to gain or deserve for one's labor or as a result of one's behavior.

Lazy Talk Word:
Ekow – to hear something twice or more which is the same.

Proper Talk Word:
Echo – repetition of a sound by reflection of sound waves; a sound produced; to resound with an echo; reverberate; to imitate.

Lazy Talk Word:
Edyoucate – to be taught knowledge or intelligence.

Proper Talk Word:
Educate – to provide with knowledge, especially through formal schooling; teach.

Lazy Talk Word:
Ephort – an attempt; an achievement.

Proper Talk Word:
Effort – the use of physical or mental energy; exertion.

Lazy Talk Word:
Egowe – to be conceited.

Proper Talk Word:
Ego – the self; egotism.

Lazy Talk Word:
Elaberate – planned with attention to detail.

Proper Talk Word:
Elaborate – complicated; to work out in detail; develop thoroughly.

Lazy Talk Word:
Elekt – to select anything by voting.

Proper Talk Word:
Elect – to select especially by being chosen from a vote.

Lazy Talk Word:
Electrawnics - a computer, cell phone, tablet, ipad, any smart device.

Proper Talk Word:
Electronics – the commercial industry of electronic devices and systems.

Lazy Talk Word:
Elowqueshun – the art of formal public speaking.

Proper Talk Word:
Elocution – a style or manner of speaking.

Lazy Talk Word:
Eloosesadate – to clarify.

Proper Talk Word:
Elucidate – to make plain and in detail.

Lazy Talk Word:
Imbellish – the best beautiful; adore someone or something.

Proper Talk Word:
Embelish – to make more
beautiful; adorn; add
details to.

Lazy Talk Word:
Imboss – to cover with a
raised design.

Proper Talk Word:
Emboss – to put something
over top of a 2d or 3d
designed item or material.

Lazy Talk Word:
Imbrayse – to hug; to accept
eagerly.

Proper Talk Word:
Embrace – to include;
to adopt as a cause; an
affectionate gesture.

Lazy Talk Word:
Imbreeowe – an organism
in its earliest stages of
development.

Proper Talk Word:
Embryo – an egg developed
in the ovaries in the
beginning stages.

Lazy Talk Word:
Emagreat – to leave
from one country, then
settledown into another
country.

Proper Talk Word:
Emigrate – to go from
country to country to
become a citizen eventually.

Lazy Talk Word:
Indoe – blunt; joint.

Proper Talk Word:
Endoe – marijuana; reefa.

Lazy Talk Word:
Indoorse – to write one's
signature on the back of a
check, stock certificate, etc.

Proper Talk Word:
Endorse – to approve;
sanction.

Lazy Talk Word:
Injanear – to plan or
accomplish by skillful acts
or contrivance.

Proper Talk Word:
Engineer – one skilled
at engineering; one who
operates an engine.

Lazy Talk Word:
Invieyournmentalelist – a person that protects the natural environment.
Proper Talk Word:
Environmentalist – one that advocates protection of the natural environment.

Lazy Talk Word:
Ecwasion – an algebraic problem that is solved through several steps to complete for to receive a final answer.
Proper Talk Word:
Equation – a math statement that 2 quantities are equal.

Lazy Talk Word:
Esquart – a quart in size of a liquid of any such; a name of a car made by Ford; a way a shofar transport one or more people to and from a destination.
Proper Talk Word:
Escort – a person, vehicle, or group accompanying another for protection or as a mark of rank; is not paid to have sex; a woman or a man who is hired to go with someone to a social event.

Lazy Talk Word:
Aspecially – talking about a specific person, place or thing.
Proper Tal Word:
Especially – used to single out one person, thing, situation over all others.

Lazy Talk Word:
Your rowe – money used in europe.
Proper Talk Word:
Euro – european money; the root word of a country – europe; a persons' name.

Lazy Talk Word:
Ezactly – to be straight forward; to a "T"; on point.
Proper Talk Word:
Exactly – to be on top of things; 100% true facts

Lazy Talk Word:
Exsirpt – a statement that is restated from a

speech, book, movie, play, music, etc.

Proper Talk Word:
Excerpt – a passage selected from a speech, book, etc.

Lazy Talk Word:
Exscershun – a name of a car; to excuse yourself; an outing.
Proper Talk Word:
Excursion – a short journey or pleasure trip.

Lazy Talk Word:
Exswiset – delicately beautiful.
Proper Talk Word:
Exquisite – sensitive; discriminating; keen; intense.

Lazy Talk Word:
Exzooberant – to have the most fun in a positive way.
Proper Talk Word:
Exuberant – full of high spirits.

(F)

Lazy Talk Word:
Fashous – joking.
Proper Talk Word:
Facetious – treating serious issues with deliberately inappropriate humor; flippant.

Lazy Talk Word:
Faque – something that is true; reality.
Proper Talk Word:
Fact – humorous.

Lazy Talk Word:
Fare – beautiful; a gathering to purchase or sell goods; doing the right thing (compromise).
Proper Talk Word:
Fair – lovely; sunny; light in color, as hair, just; equitable; moderately good; a gathering for buying and selling goods.

Lazy Talk Word:
Fayeth – trust; religious state of mind; Christian.

Proper Talk Word:
Faith – a confident belief; trust; religious convictions; loyalty; allegiance; believing in God and anything that can be believable.

Lazy Talk Word:
Fayme – public esteem; famous.
Proper Talk Word:
Fame – renown; rich and famous folk; entertainment.

Lazy Talk Word:
Fasanate – to attract irresistibly.
Proper Talk Word:
Facinate – to attract and hold attentively by a unique power, personal charm unusual nature, or some other special quality; enthrall.

Lazy Talk Word:
Fake ass – someone being two-faced; phoney.
Proper Talk Word:
False person – someone that lie; to exaggerate.

Lazy Talk Word:
Factsimalee – an exact copy or reproduction.
Proper Talk Word:
Fasimile – an exact copy, especially of written or printed material.

Lazy Talk Word:
Foepass – social problems.
Proper Talk Word:
Faux Pas – a social blunder.

Lazy Talk Word:
Fooche – an outstanding achievement.
Proper Talk Word:
Feat – a remarkable achievement.

Lazy Talk Word:
Footure – the main presentation at a motion picture theater; a characteristic.
Proper Talk Word:
Feature – the shape or aspect of the face; any distinctive characteristic; an article in a newspaper or periodical; prominent.

Lazy Talk Word:
Feedoorah – a soft felt hat.
Proper Talk Word:
Fedora – a low, soft felt hat with a curled brim and the crown creased lengthwise.

Lazy Talk Word:
Feel me – I like what vibes you have; I understand you.
Proper Talk Word:
Feeling me – to have a factual oppression that is loveable.

Lazy Talk Word:
Faine – to pretend.
Proper Talk Word:
Feign – to pretend to be affected by a feeling, state, or injury.

Lazy Talk Word:
Fellte – a fabric of matted compressed fibers of wool, fur, etc; to feel.
Proper Talk Word:
Felt – a kind of cloth made by rolling and pressing wool or another suitable textile accompanied by the application of moisture or heat, which causes the constituent fibers to mat together to create a smooth surface.

Lazy Talk Word:
Furvint – showing deep emotion. (Note: see in-depth).
Proper Talk Word:
Fervent – showing deep earnest feelings.

Lazy Talk Word:
Phet – an elaborate party (festival).
Proper Talk Word:
Fete – a festival.

Lazy Talk Word:
Fenishe – to complete anything.
Proper Talk Word:
Finish – to terminate; to complete a task; to use up; to have a conclusion of something; the end.

Lazy Talk Word:
Floorishe – to grow well.

Proper Talk Word*:*
Flourish – to thrive; to
make bold, sweeping
movements; a dramatic
action or gesture.

Lazy Talk Word:
Phoegot – can't remember;
small memory problem.
Proper Talk Word:
Forgot – to neglect or
forget.

Lazy Talk Word:
Fore-in – a county you are
not from or reside in.
Proper Talk Word:
Foreign – of or from
a country other than
one's own.

Lazy Talk Word:
Foe real – seriously;
shocked about something;
something right or original.
Proper Talk Word:
For real – factual
information; occurring
in facts; not imagined or
supposed; existing; actual
rather than imaginary, ideal

or fictitious; a story taken
from real life.

Lazy Talk Word:
Fort – a fight between
Tyson & Holyifield; to
rumble; a military base.
Proper Talk Word:
Fought – a battle or combat;
a warrior; to fight someone
personally or professionally.

Lazy Talk Word:
Fourtay – to be played
loudly and forcefully; a car
name.
Proper Talk Word:
Forte – something in which
one excels; a car, a number.

Lazy Talk Word:
Fourthrite – straight
forward; frank.
Proper Talk Word:
Forthright – a person or
their manner or speech
direct and outspoken;
straight forward and honest.

Lazy Talk Word:
Foxey – sly; slick.

Proper Talk Word:
Foxy – sly; clever.

Lazy Talk Word:
Franque – direct; to send mail free of charge; a persons' name; root word to a country's name.

Proper Tal Word:
Frank – open, honest, and direct in speech or writing, especially when dealing with unpalatable matters.

Lazy Talk Word:
Frite – the transportation of goods.

Proper Talk Word:
Freight – goods carried by a vehicle; cargo; the charge for transporting such goods.

Lazy Talk Word:
Fren – a person you know, like and trust.

Proper Talk Word:
Friend – a person whom one knows and with whom one has a bond of mutual affection, typically exclusive of sexual or family relations.

Lazy Talk Word:
Fucq – what in the world; a curse word; to have hard core sex.

Proper Talk Word:
Fuck – profanity; to be upset about something; sexual intercourse.

Lazy Talk Word:
Furer – a state of intense excitement.

Proper Talk Word:
Furor – an outbreak of public anger or excitement.

Lazy Talk Word:
Firtive – to be or act slick.

Proper Talk Word:
Furtive – stealthy; sly.

Lazy Talk Word:
Fewton – a foldable, cotton-filled mattress laid on the bed with legs to bed on floor.

Proper Talk Word:
Futon – a Japanese quilted mattress rolled out on the floor for use as a bed; a type of low wooden sofa that

can be unfolded for use as a bed.

(G)

Lazy Talk Word:
Gaph – an iron hook used to land large fish.
Proper Talk Word:
Gaff – a stick with a hook or barbed spear, for landing large fish.
Lazy Talk Word:
Geight – a way of walking and/or running.
Proper Talk Word:
Gait – a persons' manner of walking.

Lazy Talk Word:
Gamball – to bet money on a game of choice.
Proper Talk Word:
Gamble – to play a game with having chance; a bet; a risk.

Lazy Talk Word:
Gaimsmenship – the practice of winning at something by using

unethical, but not illegal means.
Proper Talk Word:
Gamesmanship – the art of winning games by using various ploys and tactics to gain a psychological advantage.

Lazy Talk Word:
Gameet – a reproduction of cells; a mature sperm or egg.
Proper Talk Word:
Gamete – a mature haploid male or female germ cell which is able to unite with another of the opposite sex in sexual reproduction to form a zygote.

Lazy Talk Word:
Garerason – a military post; a root word to – cason, kason, mason, gary, garry, etc.
Proper Talk Word:
Garrison – the troops stationed in fortress or town to defend it; to provide a place with a body of troops.

Lazy Talk Word:
Garrooluss – talking a
whole lot.
Proper Talk Word:
Garrulous – talking too
much.

Lazy Talk Word:
Gastowonamey – the art of
good eating.
Proper Talk Word:
Gastronomy – the practice
or art of choosing, cooking,
and eating good food.

Lazy Talk Word:
Jeanieolagie – a record of
ancestry.
Proper Talk Word:
Genealogy – style of
ancestry.

Lazy Talk Word:
Jenie'al – cheerful and
friendly.
Proper Talk Word:
Genial – of or relating to
marriage or generation;
favorable to growth or
comfort; marked by or
freely expressing sympathy
or friendliness.

Lazy Talk Word:
Jeanyus – great intellectual
and creative power.
Proper Talk Word:
Genius – a person who is
exceptionally intelligent or
creative, either generally or
in some particular respect.

Lazy Talk Word:
Jenshun – a plant with
showy blue flowers.
Proper Talk Word:
Gentian – a plant of
temperate and mountainous
regions, typically with
violet or vivid blue trumpet-
shaped flowers.

Lazy Talk Word:
Jenyoufleck – to bend the
knee, as in worship.
Proper Talk Word:
Genuflect – lower one's
body briefly by bending
one knee to the ground,
typically in worship or as a
sign of respect.

Lazy Talk Word:
Jenyouwin – real; frank.

Proper Talk Word:
Genuine – not artificial; to have something that is real.

Lazy Talk Word:
Geeopgraffie – the study of the earth and its features, including human life.

Proper Talk Word:
Geography – the study of the physical features of the earth and its atmosphere, and of human activity as it affects and is affected by these, including the distribution of populations and resources, land use, and industries.

Lazy Talk Word:
Geologie – the scientific study of the origin, history, and structure of the earth.

Proper Talk Word:
Geology – the science that deals with the earth's physical structure and substance, it's history, and the processes that act on it.

Lazy Talk Word:
Jermain – to the point.

Proper Talk Word:
Germane – relevant to a subject under consideration.

Lazy Talk Word:
Guyza – a hot spring that ejects a column of water.

Proper Talk Word:
Geyser – a hot spring in which water intermittently boils, sending a tall column of water and steam into the air.

Lazy Talk Word:
Gettow ebonicks – lazy talk.

Proper Talk Word:
Ghetto Ebonics – black speech.

Lazy Talk Word:
Gilled – to cover with a thin layer of gold; a part of a fish; a persons' name; a root word to gild.

Proper Talk Word:
Gild – cover thinly with gold; give a specious or false brilliance to.

Lazy Talk Word:
Gimme – to give someone
something; give me that.
Proper Talk Word:
Give me that – to share or
give someone something.

Lazy Talk Word:
Glistin – to shine; to gleam.
Proper Talk Word:
Glisten – of something
wet or greasy; a sparkling
light reflected from
something wet.

Lazy Talk Word:
Gloomeng – twilight.
Proper Talk Word:
Gloaming – dusk

Lazy Talk Word:
Gode – spur.
Proper Talk Word:
Goad – a stick used for
producing animals.

Lazy Talk Word:
Lord – the creator and ruler
of the world in monotheistic
religion; Jesus Christ,
Jehovah, etc.

Proper Talk Word:
God – a supernatural being
worshiped by a people; the
creator of the world.

Lazy Talk Word:
Gowe Gowe – relating to
disco or the music played
there.
Proper Talk Word:
Go-Go – a persons' nick
name; a type of music
name; a place to go to for to
dance and gather.

Lazy Talk Word:
Gone head – go somewhere
I ain't at; go be first.
Proper Talk Word:
Go on ahead – I don't care
if you first; so what.

Lazy Talk Word:
Gotchu – I stand behind
you 100%.
Proper Talk Word:
Got you – I will help
support you in every way.

Lazy Talk Word:
Govna – the chief executive
of a state.

Proper Talk Word:
Governor – the elected executive head of a state of the United States.

Lazy Talk Word:
Grainnight – a common, hard rock used for building.

Proper Talk Word:
Granite – a very hard, granular, crystalline, igneous rock consisting mainly of quartz, mica, and feldspar and often used as a building stone.

Lazy Talk Word:
Greatfull – thankful; gratitude.

Proper Talk Word:
Grateful – appreciating; to be thanking.

Lazy Talk Word:
Graey – a color between black and white; a name.

Proper Talk Word:
Grey – a color neutral tone between black and white, and can be used to convey gloom and dullness; color of an old photograph; a movie name; a persons' name.

Lazy Talk Word:
Graehownd – a large slender running dog; public bus that takes you within all the United States only.

Proper Talk Word:
Greyhound – a dog of a tall, slender breed having keen sight and capable of high speed, used since ancient times for hunting small game and now chiefly in racing and coursing; a national public bus transportation that travel through the whole United States.

(H)

Lazy Talk Word:
Hakka – one that breaks inside without the say so of owner to steal – information, goods, merchandise, etc; and inexperienced individual that steals from another

person; a person that finds you through digital computerized network to remotely help you.

Proper Talk Word:
Hacker – one that hacks; one who is inexperienced or inept at something; a computer enthusiast.

Lazy Talk Word:
Haknee – a horse for riding.
Proper Talk Word:
Hackney – a carriage for to hire a person for transportation of people as a business.

Lazy Talk Word:
Haleelooyah – to praise or to rejoice.
Proper Talk Word:
Hallelujah – an expression that is of praising and rejoicing.

Lazy Talk Word:
Hawlmarque – a stamp of quality on gold or silver articles; a store that sells cards and other stuff.

Proper Talk Word:
Hallmark – a mark stamped on articles of gold, silver, or platinum in Britian, certifying their standard of purity.

Lazy Talk Word:
Hawlyawd – a rope used to raise a sail, flag, etc.
Proper Talk Word:
Halyard – a rope or tackle for hoisting and lowering something (such as sails).

Lazy Talk Word:
Hayum – the thigh of the hind leg of a hog; a hogmog meat.
Proper Talk Word:
Ham – meat from the upper part of a pig's leg salted and dried or smoked; meat from a hog; actor being exaggerated on set; a licensed operator of an amateur radio station.

Lazy Talk Word:
Hangin' out – to chill or party with friends.

Proper Talk Word:
Hang out – to hang with friends or family; to have a social gathering.

Lazy Talk Word:
Hann – the part of the body that is connected to your arm, wrist, and fingers.

Proper Talk Word:
Hand – Round of applause, part of the arm below the wrist.

Lazy Talk Word:
Hannsum – pleasing and dignified in appearance.

Proper Talk Word:
Handsome – a good looking man.

Lazy Talk Word:
Happanen – an event; to play.

Proper Talk Word:
Happening – an occurrence.

Lazy Talk Word:
Hatte – material listic branded clothing for to cover the head.

Proper Talk Word:
Hat – a covering for the head with a brim.

Lazy Talk Word:
Hawtey – To be haunted by, a haunted house for a Halloween celebration.

Proper Talk Word:
Haughty/Haughton – To be haunted by, haunted house game, Aaliyah middle name; to be proud to the point of arrogance.

Lazy Talk Word:
Heresaid – Gossip between two or more individuals about information not to be 100% known as factual information.

Proper Talk Word:
Hearsay – someone talking about a topic of someone and they are not present to defend themselves.

Lazy Talk Word:
Hawrt – To feel about someone or something within your soul. The organ in your body that cause the

blood to flow for oxygen to breath.

Proper Talk Word:
Heart – The organ that pumps blood into the arteries; emotions, affection, compassion, etc.

Lazy Talk Word:
Hevin – the sky or the universe as seen from the earth; God's abode; the root word for Kevin or Levin.

Proper Talk Word:
Heaven – A place or thing that affords supreme happiness; the place the soul goes to after death.

Lazy Talk Word:
Heffa – Large and powerful; a person that is sluggish.

Proper Talk Word:
Hefta – Heavy; A young cow.

Lazy Talk Word:
Hellnaw – absolutely no.

Proper Talk Word:
Hell no – truly no.

Lazy Talk Word:
Hinchman – a person that you completely can trust that likes to do the same as you.

Proper Talk Word:
Henchman – a trusted follower; twins doing the same thing; fake twins which are look alike but not a twin doing the same thing.

Lazy Talk Word:
Hairolde – whiting hair from old age; a person that can predict the future.

Proper Talk Word:
Herald – one who proclaims important news or gives indication of something to come.

Lazy Talk Word:
Hurring – a type of fish from the oceans that goes indepth in the ocean.

Proper Talk Word:
Herring – a food fish of the Atlantic waters.

Lazy Talk Word:
Who – a person or an animal; something being cut with something larger than a knife.
Proper Talk Word:
Hew – to shape or cut down with an ax.

Lazy Talk Word:
Haya – used for haunted houses with scarecrows; a way of calling someone to get their attention.
Proper Talk Word:
Hey – used to attract attention.

Lazy Talk Word:
Hye – a formal gesture spoken to show courtesy to someone.
Proper Talk Word:
Hi – an expressive of greeting.

Lazy Talk Word:
Halareous – very funny and humorous.
Proper Talk Word:
Hilarious – boisteriously funny.

Lazy Talk Word:
Hisspannick – relating to Mexicans & Brazilians culture.
Proper Talk Word:
Hispanic – Related to Spanish or Spain speaking individuals.

Lazy Talk Word:
Hole up – a cool word for when you are trying to get someone attention; or when you ready to get in an argument this word is used; wait for a minute.
Proper Talk Word:
Hold up – stop what you doing or thinking for at least one second or more; stay here for a second more.

Lazy Talk Word:
Holla – to talk loud; talk to someone; a cool word for when leaving or before hanging up the phone; hello; goodbye; to get loud while talking; bye; bye-bye.

Proper Talk Word:
Holler – to yell or shout;
to get a loud voice that is
louder than normal when
saying something.

Lazy Talk Word:
Onnis – to be not deceptive;
the opposite of being a liar;
to be frank or sincere.
Proper Talk Word:
Honest – to be truthful,
trustworthy, and frank/
sincere.

Lazy Talk Word:
Hugh – to wrap arms
around another for a
few seconds for to show
respects; a person's name.
Proper Talk Word:
Hug – to keep close to; a
prefix to someone's name;
to clasp, embrace.

Lazy Talk Word:
Whomer – to be laughable
extremely.
Proper Talk Word:
Humor – the quality of
being comical; the ability to
perceive, enjoy, etc.

(I)

Lazy Talk Word:
I'ma – I am ready to do
something.
Proper Talk Word:
I am – you as in yourself
is ready to do or say
something.

Lazy Talk Word:
Eyese – water which is
frozen, what you use for
to see.
Proper Talk Word:
Ice – frozen water; a
person's name.

Lazy Talk Word:
[Just] ice-kareem – a
person's name, the flavored
iced desert made from dairy
products.
Proper Talk Word:
[Just] ice-cream – a desert
of flavored ice and dairy
products.

Lazy Talk Word:
Iktheology – to have factual
information about fish.
Property Talk Word:

Ichthyology – the study of fish.

Lazy Talk Word:
Ignant – very rude; a figure of speech saying you silly.
Proper Talk Word:
Ignorant – lacking knowledge when talking or conversating.

Lazy Talk Word:
Illoomanate – to clearly specify.
Proper Talk Word:
Illuminate – to clarify.

Lazy Talk Word:
Illustreus – to be a person making millions.
Proper Talk Word:
Illustrious – Famous.

Lazy Talk Word:
Emminse – Big.
Proper Talk Word:
Immense – Huge.

Lazy Talk Word:
Emmagreat – non citizens that are in another country not of their citizenship.

Proper Talk Word:
Immigrate – to settle in a foreign country.

Lazy Talk Word:
Emportint – to have power or control.
Proper Talk Word:
Important – noteworthy; significant.

Lazy Talk Word:
Empresario – the person that is the reason for production at an opera concert/show.
Proper Talk Word:
Impresario – a producer or director of an opera.

Lazy Talk Word:
Encredable – the best, spectacular.
Proper Talk Word:
Incredible – remarkable, awesome.

Lazy Talk Word:
Endepp – deep; to be advanced in something or someone.

Proper Talk Word:
In-depth – deep; to be very carefully and fully into something or someone.

Lazy Talk Word:
Endistrie – Due diligence; a specific branch of manufacture and trade.
Proper Talk Word:
Industry – the production of goods.

Lazy Talk Word:
Enflewance – a person that has either a good or bad impression on someone or something.
Proper Talk Word:
Influence – a person or thing exercising such power.

Lazy Talk Word:
Anishall – the letter of first and/or last name for verification purposes of something, which is done in cursive handwriting; first person to make or do something or create something or someone.

Proper Talk Word:
Initial – occurring first; to sign with the first letter to first and last name.

Lazy Talk Word:
Innascent – to be of truth, to not lie.
Proper Talk Word:
Innocent – to be not guilty.

Lazy Talk Word:
Insiddeus – to be sly.
Proper Talk Word:
Insidious – to be slick.

Lazy Talk Word:
Instruck – to teach and to be taught.
Proper Talk Word:
Instruct – to give and/or teach knowledge to.

Lazy Talk Word:
Intriss – to like something in-depth; a charge from a financial loan, e-bond, i-bond, bank cd, life insurance, etc.
Proper Talk Word:
Interest – a feeling of fascination; a charge for

a financial loan, e-bond, i-bond, bank cd, life insurance, etc.

Lazy Talk Word:
Intamitt – of love or sexual relations.
Proper Talk Word:
Intimate – close or familiar; personal and romantic times with someone.

Lazy Talk Word:
Inta – go inside something; to be inside.
Proper Talk Word:
Into – go inside something.

Lazy Talk Word:
Invin – to create something that is unique that can be new to others
Proper Talk Word:
Invent – to originate.

Lazy Talk Word:
Earragate – something like a well that gives out water.
Proper Talk Word:
Irrigate – to supply with water.

Lazy Talk Word:
Eyeland – a place with a large body of water surrounding it for to vacate or retire.
Proper Talk Word:
Island – a land surrounded by water.

(J)

Lazy Talk Word:
Jaqpotte – to hit the lottery or have a large advanced trophy or some type of reward.
Proper Talk Word:
Jackpot – to win a prize or reward.

Lazy Talk Word:
Jaide – a person's name; a diamond form that can be colors green or white.
Proper Talk Word:
Jade – a hard gemstone that is pale green or white.

Lazy Talk Word:
Jarging – a different type of language spoken that

doesn't have full proper pronunciation of word or can have the proper pronunciation on purpose.

Proper Talk Word:
Jargon – specialized language of a group, profession, etc.

Lazy Talk Word:
Johntee – to give dap to; self-confident.

Proper Talk Word:
Jaunty – dapper; carefree.

Lazy Talk Word:
Jellee Fiche – microfiche; a jelly like sea animal that stings extremely if human has contact with it.

Proper Talk Word:
Jellyfish – a gelatinous, umbrella shaped sea animal.

Lazy Talk Word:
Juwell – a body ornament with lots of value, such as a gold carved into a specific type of shape or diamonds; prefix of a person's name.

Proper Talk Word:
Jewel – a gem or diamond; a treasured person or thing.

Lazy Talk Word:
Jurey – diamonds, rings, necklaces, bracelets; jewelry.

Proper Talk Word:
Jewelry – karat gold; stainless steel; sterling silver; platinum; diamonds; bronze jewelry.

Lazy Talk Word:
Gigge – to dance with heart and soul.

Proper Talk Word:
Jig/Jigger – A lively dance; small measure for liquor, usually 1.5 ounces.

Lazy Talk Word:
Gingal – a tingly sound; Christmas music.

Proper Talk Word:
Jingle – a simple, catchy rhyme; a type of music.

Lazy Talk Word:
Gobb – a place for to have a business transaction completed with employees,

supervisors and a chain of command.

Proper Talk Word:
Job – an activity performed for payment.

Lazy Talk Word:
Gogg – to move legs forward with a force of speed that is faster than walking.

Proper Talk Word:
Jog – jolt/nudge; run at a steady trot.

Lazy Talk Word:
Jownt – when two different things are put together to form as one; weed; the space between the two bones conjoined.

Proper Talk Word:
Joint – a point where as though 2 or more things are joined; a marijuana blunt; connection between movable bodily parts.

Lazy Talk Word:
Joken – to say something very hilarious.

Proper Talk Word:
Joking – one who tells or play a monologue that is very funny and/or humorous.

Lazy Talk Word:
Jyelee – merry; festive; a piece of delicious sour candy that is rectangular shaped.

Proper Talk Word:
Jolly – to feel really excited; to be of the Christmas spirit; candy rapped into place twisted with a rectangular shape.

Lazy Talk Word:
Jawsh – to tease something extremely.

Proper Talk Word:
Josh – to joke very adamantly.

Lazy Talk Word:
Jonesing – telling a humorous joke on something or someone, in a laughing matter; a person's name; making jokes about

someone in a laughing matter.

Proper Talk Word:

Jones in – a person's name; to tell a joke about someone or something for purposes of laughing and have a good time; pointing out good or bad things about someone or something in a joking manner; a fixation on or compulsive desire for someone or something, such as: a drug or an addiction.

Lazy Talk Word:

Jurnalism – to publish a story, large or small in news periodicals; to keep track of day to day activities; a nike diary book.

Proper Talk Word:

Journalism – the collecting, writing, editing and publishing of news in periodicals.

Lazy Talk Word:

Jurnie - to take a vacation anywhere that is considered to be traveling.

Proper Talk Word:

Journey - to travel or take a trip anywhere.

Lazy Talk Word:

Julius – a character spelled slightly different from the play Romeo and Juliet created by William Shakespeare; a person's name.

Proper Talk Word:

Juliet – a character in the play Romeo and Juliet by William Shakespeare.

Lazy Talk Word:

Jirisproodence – the science of law; a legal system.

Proper Talk Word:

Jurisprudence - the theory or philosophy of law; a legal system.

Lazy Talk Word:

Justus – To be fair; a person's name; a name of a movie; a name of a character in a movie; to receive a legal case judgment; a tag name on

a car; just you and me;
the law.

Proper Talk Word:
Justice – Fairness; moral
rightness; a person's name;
name of a movie or show;
kid's clothing name brand;
the law a name of actor
or actress; to be free of
anything "good or bad".

(K)

Lazy Talk Word:
Care-it – the style of a
specific type of real gold
karat ring.

Proper Talk Word:
Karat – a measure of 24
units used for to proportion
the pure gold in an alloy.

Lazy Talk Word:
Keowe plan – the type
of money left in for a
retirement plan.

Proper Talk Word:
Keogh plan – a retirement
plan for the self-employed.

Lazy Talk Word:
Keptee – a type of hat
that is worn by the French
military.

Lazy Talk Word:
Kepi – a French military
cap with a flat, circular top
and a visor.

Lazy Talk Word:
Kilowachs – watts that
equal to 1000 watts; a
person's name.

Proper Talk Word:
Kilowatts – one thousand
watts.

Lazy Talk Word:
Kang – a royal individual; a
playing card with a picture
of a royal individual that is
the Father of the Prince and
Husband to the Queen.

Proper Talk Word:
King – a male monarch;
a playing card bearing a
picture of a royal individual
that is the Father of the
Prince and Husband to the
Queen.

Lazy Talk Word:
Kicse – to use your mouth to touch another persons' lips or body; brand name candy called Kiss; used to greet a significant other.
Proper Talk Word:
Kiss – to touch with lips in an affectionate way, or to greet someone with, etc; a small piece of chocolate candy.

Lazy Talk Word:
Cit – an equipment instrument; parts that need be put together.
Proper Talk Word:
Kit – A set of instruments or equipment.

Lazy Talk Word:
Neal – a person's name; to bow down on the center part of a leg; to propose to in a sort of fashion.
Proper Talk Word:
Kneel – to rest or bent legs while mostly pressure on the center of the leg which is the knee.

Lazy Talk Word:
Nite – a time of the day; a movie titled "The Black Knight".
Proper Talk Word:
Knight – a medieval gentleman soldier; the holder of a nonhereditary title conferred by a sovereign; to raise to knighthood.

Lazy Talk Word:
Nylidge – to be intelligent; smart.
Proper Talk Word:
Knowledge – to learn; to be familiar; or to be aware.

Lazy Talk Word:
Cumkwot – a fruit that tastes just like an orange.
Proper Talk Word:
Kumquat – a small, edible orangelike fruit.

(L)

Lazy Talk Word:
Layball – a white or colored sticker that can have text

input on it to recognize what a specific item is for in an inventory of such.

Proper Talk Word:
Label - a tag attached to an article designate its owner, contents, etc.

Lazy Talk Word:
Lagune – a part of the land that is separated between the sea, sand and/or reefs.

Proper Talk Word:
Lagoon – a body of brackish water separated from the sea by sandbars or reefs.

Lazy Talk Word:
Lanae – to arrive or cause to arrive by airplane or car; to have great landscaping within the land; a person's name.

Proper Talk Word:
Land – the solid part of the earth's surface; a portion or region of this; to land at a certain place.

Lazy Talk Word:
Lanaelady – the female that owns or rent property.

Proper Talk Word:
Landlady – a woman who owns and leases property.

Lazy Talk Word:
Lanaelord – a male that owns or rent property.

Proper Talk Word:
Landlord – a man who owns and leases property.

Lazy Talk Word:
Lanae – a street is narrow from left to right and long frontwards and backwards.

Proper Talk Word:
Lane – a narrow way or road.

Lazy Talk Word:
Lappizlazoolee – a in-depth blue gemstone; people born in December birthstone.

Proper Talk Word:
Lapislazuli – deep blue gemstone that is opaque.

Lazy Talk Word:
Lawd – to praise or command; all glory, laud and honor to Thee.

Proper Talk Word:
Laud - an office of solemn praise to God forming with matins the first of the canonical hours.

Lazy Talk Word:
Laff – to be hilarious with an exciting facial expression; a name to a candy.
Proper Talk Word:
Laugh – to produce sound of having joy; to be humorously funny with a facial expression to show how you feel inside.

Lazy Talk Word:
Lauw a rule established by authority, society, or custom.
Proper Talk Word:
Law – a body of such rules; the profession relating to such rules; a generalization based on observed phenomena.

Lazy Talk Word:
Lawya – a person that has a law degree for to represent an acused in the court of law or other business entities, etc.
Proper Talk Word:
Lawyer – a professional who practices law; an attorney.

Lazy Talk Word:
Layzee – don't feel like doing something; to be slow to move due to feelings of being slightly tired; to pronounce sluggishly (lazy).
Proper Talk Word:
Lazy – indolent, slothful; slow-moving sluggish pronunciation of a word, sentence, or paragraph, etc.
Lazy Talk Word:
Lede – to guide, conduct, escort someone to a destination requested; or to direct someone at a specific destination; to escort someone in a classroom by showing them in steps by giving several different types of clues for to enforce the escortee to obtain or get an answer to a questions and/or situation.

Proper Talk Word:
Lead – to be ahead or at the head of; to pursue; to live; to have first place at anything; the main part in a play, movie etc.

Lazy Talk Word:
Levar – a person's name; to have permission to leave a duty; a type of green plant that is flat with vines in it; farewell.

Proper Talk Word:
Leaves – to go elsewhere; a person's name; green flattened plant structure attached to a stem; thin sheet of gold; permission to be absent from duty; to let or cause to remain; to depart; to bequeath.

Lazy Talk Word:
Lagittamit – lawful, authentic, and reasonable.

Proper Talk Word:
Legitimate – genuine; conforming to the law or to rules.

Lazy Talk Word:
Lamoetive – a dominant and recurring theme.

Proper Talk Word:
Leitmotif – a melodic passage or phrase associated with a particular character.

Lazy Talk Word:
Limming – a specific species that is located in the European sea that is a mass migration.

Proper Talk Word:
Lemming – a species of European rodent notorious for its mass migrations into the sea.

Lazy Talk Word:
Limman – a sour tasteful fruit when combined with sugar with the juices squeezed into a container will create lemon juice.

Proper Talk Word:
Lemon – a yellow citrus fruit with sour, juicy pulp; a type of a tattoo.

Lazy Talk Word:

Lyca – to put your mouth on something passionately; to lick someone or something.

Proper Talk Word:

Lick[a] – to smooch with lips on another or something; to kiss someone or something.

Lazy Talk Word:

Lykken – a person's name; to have mutual feelings for someone.

Proper Talk Word

Like in – to want someone or have possession of someone or something; the way a heart feels about someone or something.

Lazy Talk Word:

Limarick – a person's name; a poem with five lines that is very hilarious.

Proper Talk Word:

Limerick – a humorous 5-line poem.

Lazy Talk Word:

Limoezeen – a large vehicle that carry a minimum of 5 people in, with a built-in bar and a sun roof, used to escort a person from one destination to the final destination.

Proper Talk Word:

Limousine – an escort vehicle used to escort a person from one destination to their final destination; a large passenger vehicle driven by a chauffeur.

Lazy Talk Word:

Lingwistix – the study of language.

Proper Talk Word:

Linguistics – the science of language.

Lazy Talk Word:

Lissen – to pay attention to; to hear something.

Proper Talk Word:

Listen – To make an effort to hear something.

Lazy Talk Word:

Lyegick – valid reasoning.

Proper Talk Word:
Logic – the study of reasoning.

Lazy Talk Word:
Lewce – not tighly fitted; to slack.

Proper Talk Word:
Loose – immoral; not literal or exact; to make less tight or firm.

Lazy Talk Word:
Luv – a feeling of emotion that can be little of a lot of how you feel about someone or something; to show romance; to show passion; to care for deeply for someone; a tattoos name or meaning.

Proper Talk Word:
Love – an intense affectionate concern for a passionate attraction to another person; to care for someone in-depth; a person's name; a tattoo name.

Lazy Talk Word:
Loiwyul – to be faithful to someone or something; a college name.

Proper Talk Word:
Loyal – to be faithful to a someone or something.

(M)

Lazy Talk Word:
Macho – a person's name; characterized by machismo.

Proper Talk Word:
Machado – a person's name; a surname of Portuguese and Spanish origin that means "axe" or "hatchet" dating back to approximately 2nd century Europe. It is commonly found in Portugal, Spain, Brazil, Latin America, and India (southern Tamil Nadu) due to the Portuguese and Spanish colonization during the age of discovery.

<u>Lazy Talk Word</u>:
Makizmo – an exaggeration of sense of masculinity.
<u>Proper Talk Word</u>:
Machismo – means macho; strong or aggressive masculine pride.

<u>Lazy Talk Word</u>:
Ma'am – a courteous way of addressing a woman or female officer in the military.
<u>Proper Talk Word</u>:
Madam – a courteous form of address to a woman.

<u>Lazy Talk Word</u>:
Mayne – feelings of all man; an adult male human being; a board game piece; figure of speech when reached high point in a conversation.
<u>Proper Talk Word</u>:
Man – a person; the human race; a piece used in board games; to supply with men; take one's place for work at; figure of speech when reached high point in a conversation.

<u>Lazy Talk Word</u>:
Man's in nem' – a person and their friends.
<u>Proper Talk Word</u>:
Man's and them – to hang out with others.

<u>Lazy Talk Word</u>:
Maynna – a way of doing something; custom; to be polite.
<u>Proper Talk Word</u>:
Manner – one's natural bearing; polite social behavior; to be kind.

<u>Lazy Talk Word</u>:
Maynaly – politeness.
<u>Proper Talk Word</u>:
Mannerly – very nice; proper.

<u>Lazy Talk Word</u>:
Manyouscrip – a type written or hand written version of an article, book, play, or movie that can be submitted for publication.

Proper Talk Word:
Manuscript – a document written by hand; an author's text that has not yet been published.

Lazy Talk Word:
Merrithawn – a long distance race with people from all over not just Olympic people.

Proper Talk Word:
Marathon – a contest of endurance.

Lazy Talk Word:
Mariwanna – the legal medication designed to help glaucoma, depression and other illnesses; a weed plant.

Proper Talk Word:
Marijuana – the dried flowers and leaves of the hemp plant, smoked to induce euphoria.

Lazy Talk Word:
Marry-onnet – a doll that is designed to make kids laugh that is connected to strings for movement and venture.

Proper Talk Word:
Marionette – a puppet manipulated by strings.

Lazy Talk Word:
Marq – a image created and written with a pen, pencil, crayon, paint, onto a piece of paper, or other types of pads or paper designed for to be designed with different types of marks; a person's name; a happening that is unforgettable.

Proper Talk Word:
Mark – a visible impression on something, as a spot, dent, or line; a written printed symbol; a grade; a target or goal.

Lazy Talk Word:
Markey – a large sign for a store.

Proper Talk Word:
Marquee – a rooflike structure projecting over an entrance.

Lazy Talk Word:
Masta – one that is the overall boss; to be highly

advanced in a topic or subject; a type of degree program college known to be a graduate degree.
Proper Talk Word:
Master – one highly skilled; a boss; overcome or subdue; a captain of a merchant ship.

Lazy Talk Word:
Massirpeace – a painting, document, or anything that is completed with the ultimate and best results which makes it better and 1st place piece of art.
Proper Talk Word:
Masterpiece – an outstanding work of art; anything superlative.

Lazy Talk Word:
Meka – a person's name; a place that attracts people to it; the huge outlet mall near your hometown is, for shoppers and bargain hunters; when it's capitalized, it is the holiest city for Muslims, the place where Muhammad was born.
Proper Talk Word:
Mecca – the holy city of Islam; a center of interest; a person's name; a clothing name brand.

Lazy Talk Word:
Mamentoe – a souvenir; a valuable remembrance.
Proper Talk Word:
Memento – a reminder; reward or award.

Lazy Talk Word:
Murcey – kindness; clemency.
Proper Talk Word:
Mercy – a fortunate act or occurrence.

Lazy Talk Word:
Matecyoulas – extremely careful and precise.
Proper Talk Word:
Meticulous – scrupulous; showing great attention to detail.

Lazy Talk Word:
Mikeal – a Godly name; a French name.
Proper Talk Word:
Michael – means "who is like God"; a French name.

Lazy Talk Word:
Michal – means "me how"; a person's name; a Polish and Poland name; to be a Princess, Queen or King depending on the sex of the person.
Proper Talk Word:
Michelle – a person's name; a French name; a means "Michael"; no royal meaning.

Lazy Talk Word:
Mikecrowphone – an instrument for converting sound waves into electrical energy variations which may then be amplified, transmitted, or recorded.
Proper Talk Word:
Microphone – an instrument that converts sound waves into electric signals, a in broadcasting.

Lazy Talk Word:
Mister – a person's name; variant form of Mr., often used humorously or with offensive emphasis.
Proper Talk Word:
Mr. – a title preceding a man's surname.

Lazy Talk Word:
Mockason – a person's name; a soft leather slipper or shoe.
Proper Talk Word:
Moccasin - a heelless shoe made entirely of soft leather, as deerskin, with the sole brought up and attached to a piece of u-shaped leather on top of the foot, worn originally by the American Indians.

Lazy Talk Word:
Monaterry – of money.
Proper Talk Word:
Monetary - relating to money or currency.

Lazy Talk Word:
Manoppowely – a person's name; a game board game; exclusive ownership or control.

Proper Talk Word:
Monopoly – a name of a board game; a company or group having such control; a commodity or service thus controlled.

Lazy Talk Word:
Momma Kia – to be a mother to your child; a nickname from the author of this book son.

Lazy Talk Word:
Monnowetheism – to believe in one God.

Proper Talk Word:
Monotheism – the belief only there is one God.

Lazy Talk Word:
Mietow – when expressing your goals and its principles'.

Proper Talk Word:
Motto – a brief phrase used to express a principle, goal, or ideal.

Lazy Talk Word:
Moo – to change position; affect deeply; a nick name.

Proper Talk Word:
Move – to settle in a new place; to take some action; a player's turn to move a piece in a board game.

Lazy Talk Word:
Moosiq - vocal or instrumental sounds (or both) combined in such a way as to produce beauty of form, harmony, and expression of emotion.

Proper Talk Word:
Music – the art of organizing sounds to create an aesthetic combination of rhythm, melody, and harmony; the written or printed signs representing vocal or instrumental sound.

(N)

Lazy Talk Word:
Nah – can't do or say something; not at all; negative vote.
Proper Talk Word:
No (in German – Nien) – opposite of yes or go; used to express refusal; to deny something to happen or go forward.

Lazy Talk Word:
Nairrate – to tell a story; a narrator.
Proper Talk Word:
Narrate – a narrator; a story being told.

Moma Kia – a store name; a nickname from author's child of this book spelled slightly different; a parents' title with name.

Lazy Talk Word:
Nafarirs – wicked.
Proper Talk Word:
Nafarrious – wicked.

Lazy Talk Word:
Newtrall – not favoring or belonging to either side in a dispute; to be non-chalant.
Proper Talk Word:
Neutral – Indifferent; designating a color with no hue.

Lazy Talk Word:
Nicnaime – a descriptive, informal, or affectionate name used instead of a real name.
Proper Talk Word:
Nickname - a usually descriptive name given instead of or in addition to the one belonging to a person, place, or thing; a familiar form of a proper name (as of a person or a city).

Lazy Talk Word:
Knowball – to show greatness of character.
Proper Talk Word:
Noble – grand; stately; magnificent.

Lazy Talk Word:
Nominclaycha – a system of names in an art or science.
Proper Talk Word:
Nomenclature - the body or system of names in a particular field.

Lazy Talk Word:
Nyemanate – to put on a ballot for to be a political candidate.
Proper Talk Word:
Nominate – to appoint to an office, honor, political candidate, etc.

Lazy Talk Word:
Nosey – to meddle in someone else's business; or eve's drop on someone.
Proper Talk Word:
Nose [see] – to see someone's body part of the face.

Lazy Talk Word:
Noetaball – to be seen; to be remarkable.

Proper Talk Word:
Notable – worthy of notice; a person of note or distinction.

Lazy Talk Word:
Nowete – a letter written to someone; a song that has notes in it to be sung.
Proper Talk Word:
Note - a brief written record or communication; remark; a tone in musical notation; importance.

Lazy Talk Word:
Nufin – to not need or want; nothing.
Proper Talk Word:
Nothing – not interested; to not have anything.

Lazy Talk Word:
Nyvol – a book that consists of several essay paragraphs and sentences to form a story of interest for its readers.
Proper Talk Word:
Novel – a long fictional prose narrative.

Lazy Talk Word:
Nahvice - a person new to or inexperienced in a field or situation.
Proper Talk Word:
Novice – one who has entered a religious order but has not yet taken final vows; a beginner in a contest.

Lazy Talk Word:
None – to have nothing; a nun; someone that is a believer in God and lives in a religious community.
Proper Talk Word:
Nun – a woman who belongs to a religious community.

(O)

Lazy Talk Word:
Oweth – a take a vow or oath to do something.
Proper Talk Word:
Oath – a formal promise to do something.

Lazy Talk Word:
Owebae – to listen to what is right or according to any laws.
Proper Talk Word:
Obey – to do what one is ordered to do.

Lazy Talk Word:
Oktet – to sing a song that is written and designed for 8 different people or 8 different instruments.
Proper Talk Word:
Octet – a musical composition written for 8 voices or instruments.

Lazy Talk Word:
Auhde – a poem characterized by a lyric noble style.
Proper Talk Word:
Ode – a lyric poem in the form of an address to a particular subject, often elevated in style or manner and written in varied or irregular meter.
a poem meant to be sung.

Lazy Talk Word:
Offishus – giving advice to something personally and professionally; Excessively forward in offering one's services.
Proper Talk Word:
Officious - assertive of authority in an annoyingly domineering way, especially with regard to petty or trivial matters.

Lazy Talk Word:
Oh my – to be surprised someone is mocking you.
Proper Talk Word:
Oh my – to not believe it to the point you call out to God.

Lazy Talk Word:
Oh kay – to approve of; to agree to; a person's name; someone's nickname; to understand.
Proper Talk Word:
Okay – a person's name; expressive of approval or agreement; a person's way of saying they on point; to be ready.

Lazy Talk Word:
Ole' world – the E hemisphere, especially Europe.
Proper Talk Word:
Old world - belonging to or associated with former times, especially when considered quaint and attractive.

Lazy Talk Word:
Ipara - a dramatic work in one or more acts, set to music for singers and instrumentalists; a building for the performance of opera.
Proper Talk Word:
Opera – a dramatic presentation set to music.

Lazy Talk Word:
Orr – a long pole with a blade at one end, use to row a boat.
Proper Talk Word:
Oar - a pole with a flat blade, pivoting in an oar

lock, used to row or steer a boat through the water.

Lazy Talk Word:
Orgasim - a climax of sexual excitement, characterized by feelings of pleasure centered in the genitals and (in men) experienced as an accompaniment to ejaculation.
Proper Talk Word:
Orgasm – a sexual climax.

Lazy Talk Word:
Ohrigenal – to be first in order of existence; creative; an authentic work of art.
Proper Talk Word:
Original - present or existing from the beginning; first or earliest; created directly and personally by a particular artist; not a copy or imitation.

Lazy Talk Word:
Ohrigonate – to come or bring into being; begin.

Proper Talk Word:
Originate - create or initiate (something); have a specified beginning.

Lazy Talk Word:
Orenathylogy – the study of birds.
Proper Talk Word:
Ornithology - a branch of zoology dealing with birds.

(P)

Lazy Talk Word:
Paddal – a long stick (also called an oar) which is used to make the boat move by human contact pushing the waves to go forward or backward in the boat (canoe).
Proper Talk Word:
Paddle – an oar for a canoe (a small stylish boat).

Lazy Talk Word:
Panachaye – Swagger; dash; verve; flamboyant confidence of style or manner.

Proper Talk Word:
Panache – Swagger; a
tuft or plume of feathers,
especially as a headdress or
on a helmet.

Lazy Talk Word:
Paure – the interest accrued
for a stock, bond, savings
account, etc.

Proper Talk Word:
Par – the face value of a
stock, bond, etc.

Lazy Talk Word:
Porade – an assortment
of individuals performing
different style dances and
marching in the main
streets of a town for a
trophy competition based of
the body movement and the
music beats from the band.

Proper Talk Word:
Parade – a public procession
held on a ceremonial
occasion; to flaunt.

Lazy Talk Word:
Parakeat – any of numerous
usually small slender parrots
with a long-graduated tail.

Proper Talk Word:
Parakeet – a small parrot
with predominantly green
plumage and a long tail.

Lazy Talk Word:
Partin – to get a felony or
misdemeanor expunged
off of someone's criminal
record.

Proper Talk Word:
Pardon – to forgive
something or someone
as if something has never
happened.

Lazy Talk Word:
Pairrutt – a bird, brightly
colored and able to repeat
language; to repeat without
understanding.

Proper Talk Word:
Parrot – a bird having a
hooked bill, brightly colored
plumage, and sometimes
the ability to mimic speech.

Lazy Talk Word:
Pas – to proceed; to win.

Proper Talk Word:
Pass – to go by or ahead; receive an award or reward for finishing something.

Lazy Talk Word:
Pashun – sexual desire.
Proper Talk Word:
Passion – a powerful emotion or appetite.

Lazy Talk Word:
Passeda – the end; moving forward; the time before the present time.
Proper Talk Word:
Past – gone; over; happened in an early time period.

Lazy Talk Word:
Patramoeny – an inheritance; property inherited from one's father or male ancestor.
Proper TalkWord:
Patrimony - the estate or property belonging by ancient endowment or right to a church or other institution.

Lazy Talk Word:
Patruewn – a landholder in the Dutch colony of what is now New York and New Jersey.
Proper Talk Word:
Patroon - the estate or property belonging by ancient endowment or right to a church or other institution.

Lazy Talk Word:
Peece – the absence of war or hostile; to be calm; used as a friendly greeting.
Proper Talk Word:
Peace - freedom from disturbance; tranquility; used as an order to remain silent.

Lazy Talk Word:
Pinsiv – thoughtful in-depth.
Proper Talk Word:
Pensive – deeply thoughtful.

Lazy Talk Word:
Perkyoulate – to filter; a name to a dance; a person's name.

Proper Talk Word:
Perculate - (of a liquid or gas) filter gradually through a porous surface or substance; a dance; a person's name.

Lazy Talk Word:
Purmitt – a document that allows you to get something, such as a fence around a house, a driving permit id from the MVA, or a building permit for to be built.
Proper Talk Word:
Permit – a document granting permission.

Lazy Talk Word:
Percwasit – an extra amount of funds on a pay check.
Proper Talk Word
Perquisite – a bonus payment besides regular pay check.

Lazy Talk Word:
Purspectiv – a point of view.
Proper Talk Word:
Perspective – the technique of representing objects on a flat surface so that they have the 3d quality as when seen with the eye; to make a point.

Lazy Talk Word:
Purt – bold and saucy.
Proper Talk Word:
Pert – high spirited; vivacious.

Lazy Talk Word:
Peryooce – to read or examine something or someone with care.
Proper Talk Word:
Peruse - read (something), typically in a thorough or careful way.

Lazy Talk Word:
Feenix – a birth that consumes itself by 500 years and rises anew from the ashes; a person or thing regarded as uniquely remarkable in some respect.
Proper Talk Word:
Phoenix - (in classical mythology) a unique bird that lived for five or six centuries in the Arabian

desert, after this time burning itself on a funeral pyre and rising from the ashes with renewed youth to live through another cycle.

Lazy Talk Word:
Fisseyology – the science of life processes, activities, and functions.
Proper Talk Word:
Physiology - the branch of biology that deals with the normal functions of living organisms and their parts; the way in which a living organism or bodily part functions.

Lazy Talk Word:
Pyed – colors of patch; each has different color and/or designed; name of a song or person.
Proper Talk Word:
Pied – patchy in color; a person's name; a name or lyrics to a song.

Lazy Talk Word:
Pigun – a bird with a deep chested body and short legs;

a gullible person, especially someone swindled in gambling or the victim of a confidence trick.
Proper Talk Word:
Pigeon - a stout seed or fruit eating bird with a small head, short legs, and a cooing voice, typically having grey and white plumage; victim of different trick ideas and very gullible.

Lazy Talk Word:
Penque flairers – signify passion, sentiment, and love; the color is contemporary and hence, the flowers are very versatile; the blooms go on several occasions, from happiness to admiration, from love to gratitude and from showing thankfulness to convey departure.
Proper Talk Word:
Pink Flowers – the highest degree; pink with fragrant related to the carnation.

Lazy Talk Word:
Plawsable – to give the first impression of truthfulness and reasonableness.
Proper Talk Word:
Plausible – appearing true or reasonable.

Lazy Talk Word:
Plae – to have fun; take part in a game; to act in a drama or play; to look at a movie or play; to be in a sports game.
Proper Talk Word:
Play - engage in activity for enjoyment and recreation rather than a serious or practical purpose; take part in (a sport).

Lazy Talk Word:
Plae wryte – a person that writes a play; the creator of a play.
Proper Talk Word:
Playwright - a writer of plays.

Lazy Talk Word:
Ple aye – an appeal or urgent request.

Proper Talk Word:
Plea - a formal statement by or on behalf of a defendant or prisoner, stating guilt or innocence in response to a charge, offering an allegation of fact, or claiming that a point of law should apply.

Lazy Talk Word:
Plej – something given or held as security in a loan, contract, etc; to say the Pledge of Allegiance.
Proper Talk Word:
Pledge – to promise solemnly; to bind by a pledge; to deposit as security.

Lazy Talk Word:
Poe-um/Poe-atrie – a work of poetry; the art of work of a poet; to write words in the form of a sentence or paragraph that sometimes rhyme to tell a story uniquely in a specific way, depending on the style of poetry chosen.

Proper Talk Word:
Poem/Poetry – verse as distinguished from prose; a piece of writing that partakes of the nature of both speech and song that is nearly always rhythmical, usually metaphorical, and often exhibits such formal elements as meter, rhyme, and stanzaic structure; literary work in which special intensity is given to the expression of feelings and ideas by the use of distinctive style and rhythm; poems collectively or as a genre of literature.

Lazy Talk Word:
Pielasee – a written contract of insurance; policy.
Proper Talk Word:
Policy – a method or course of action followed by a government, an individual, etec.

Lazy Talk Word:
Powelish – to become smooth and shiny when brushed onto a finger nail or toenail, tires, etc; a resident or citizen of Poland; a person's name.
Proper Talk Word:
Polish – a substance used to polish a surface; of, relating to, or characteristic of Poland, the Poles, or Polish; a person's name.

Lazy Talk Word:
Powelight – having or showing good manners; courteous.
Proper Talk Word:
Polite - having or showing behavior that is respectful and considerate of other people.

Lazy Talk Word:
Polatiq's – the policies or affairs of a government; the conducting of political affairs.
Proper Talk Word:
Politics – the art of science of government; the confession of a person so involved.

Lazy Talk Word:
P.S. (Powce Scripp) – a message added at the end of a letter after the writer's signature.

Proper Talk Word:
P.S. (Post Script) - A postscript (P.S.) is an afterthought, thought that's occurring after the letter has been written and signed. The term comes from the Latin post scriptum, an expression meaning "written after" (which may be interpreted in the sense of "that which comes after the writing").

Lazy Talk Word:
Postyoulit – to assume without being able to prove it by sight or documented.

Proper Talk Word:
Postulate – to assume with no proof.

Lazy Talk Word:
Poscher – to assume an exaggerated pose; prance.

Proper Talk Word:
Posture – a characteristic way of bearing one's body; carriage.

Lazy Talk Word:
Powes – to hold a position, as in modeling.

Proper Talk Word:
Pose – to affect a particular attitude; to propound.

Lazy Talk Word:
Powwa – the ability to act effectively; authority; predominate.

Proper Talk Word:
Power – strength; the ability to exercise control; mechanical power.

Lazy Talk Word:
Praer – a solemn request for help or expression of thanks addressed to God or an object of worship.

Proper Talk Word:
Prayer – a reverant petition made to God.

Lazy Talk Word:
Prerygative - arising from the prerogative of the Crown (usually delegated to the government or the judiciary) and based in common law rather than statutory law.
Proper Talk Word:
Prerogative – an exclusive right or privilege.

Lazy Talk Word:
Prezadint – the chief executive of a republic or democrat; the President of the United States; an owner of a business.
Proper Talk Word:
President – the chief officer of a corporation; the elected head of a republican state.

Lazy Talk Word:
Propps – to give someone the benefit of the doubt.
Proper Talk Word:
Props – material or equipment for an actor, actress, staged play, or film (movie) to use for entertainment.

(Q)

Lazy Talk Word:
Cwolafy – to be or make competent for a position, office, etc; to meet the standards.
Proper Talk Word:
Qualify - be entitled to a particular benefit or privilege by fulfilling a necessary condition.

Lazy Talk Word:
Kwontatey – a number or an amount.
Proper Talk Word:
Quantity - a particular or indefinite amount of anything:

Lazy Talk Word:
Corta masta – a military officer responsible for individuals, and equipment; to be a quartermaster.

Proper Talk Word:
Quarter master - a military officer responsible for providing quarters, rations, clothing, and other supplies.

Lazy Talk Word:
Kween – the wife or widow of a King; a person's name; a card from the deck of cards; a name brand; the game piece of a board game.

Proper Talk Word:
Queen – the female ruler of an independent state, especially one who inherits the position by right of birth; the most powerful chess piece that each player has, able to move any number of unobstructed squares in any direction along a rank, file, or diagonal on which it stands.

Lazy Talk Word:
Kwote – to repeat the words of another, recite, state a price.

Proper Talk Word:
Quote - give someone (the estimated price of a job or service); to restate what another said previously while giving credit to the original person's words.

(R)

Lazy Talk Word:
Readyowe – the equipment used for transmitting or receiving radio signals; used for to listen and sing music.

Proper Talk Word:
Radio – the use of electromagnetic waves to transmit electric signals without wires; used for to hear and sing music.

Lazy Talk Word:
Reeak – to act in response to.

Proper Talk Word:
React – to be affected by circumstances.

Lazy Talk Word:
Reddy – prepared or available.

Proper Talk Word:
Ready – willing; on-point.

Lazy Talk Word:
Reeaul – authentic; existing in fact or actuality.
Proper Talk Word:
Real – genuine; actually existing as a thing or occurring in fact; not imagined or supposed.

Lazy Talk Word:
Reallaty – the state of being real; actual existence; to step out of a fairy tale that doesn't exist.
Proper Talk Word:
Reality - the world or the state of things as they actually exist, as opposed to an idealistic or notional idea of them.

Lazy Talk Word:
Relm – a Kingdom; a field of expertive or interest.
Proper Talk Word:
Realm - a primary biogeographical division of the earth's surface; a field or domain of activity or interest.

Lazy Talk Word:
Reem – a person's name; a large quantity of something, typically paper or writing on paper;
Proper Talk Word:
Ream – often; very much; a person's name; 500 (formerly 480) sheets of paper.

Lazy Talk Word:
Recapatyoulate – to summarize.
Proper Talk Word:
Recapitulate – to review.

Lazy Talk Word:
Resight – to repeat aloud something that you have memorized; recollect; to remember.
Proper Talk Word:
Recite – to emunerate.

Lazy Talk Word:
Reenforst – to support.
Proper Talk Word:
Reinforce – to strengthen.

Lazy Talk Word:
Rejoyce – to be joyful; happy.
Proper Talk Word:
Rejoice – to feel or fill with joy.

Lazy Talk Word:
Relie – to trust confidently.
Proper Talk Word:
Rely – to depend.

Lazy Talk Word:
Riemitt – to pardon or forgive.
Proper Talk Word:
Remit – to diminish; abate.

Lazy Talk Word:
Reepint – to feel regret for what one has done or failed to do; to bow to God for forgiveness about a sin committed.
Proper Talk Word:
Repent - feel or express sincere regret or remorse about one's wrongdoing or sin.

Lazy Talk Word:
Repyoutayshun – a personal background that someone is known by; actions that gives you reason to flaunt.
Proper Talk Word:
Reputation – a specific character or trait.

Lazy Talk Word:
Resaulve – to decide firmly; good intentions to fix something or someone situation.
Proper Talk Word:
Resolve – to decide by formal vote; resolution; a determination or decision.

Lazy Talk Word:
Respeck – to give honor to someone; to have esteem talking or doing something.
Proper Talk Word:
Respect - a feeling of deep admiration for someone or something elicited by their abilities, qualities, or achievements; admire (someone or something) deeply, as a result of their

abilities, qualities, or achievements.

Lazy Talk Word:
Rijj – a long, narrow land elevation.
Proper Talk Word:
Ridge – a narrow raised strip.

Lazy Talk Word:
Roberthwin – to rob someone of something; to be born to win; a person's name; a German given name that means also to be bright, famous, etc.
Proper Talk Word:
Robert – a person's name; an ancient Germanic given name, a Germanic name; "fame" and *berhta- "bright"; Old Dutch; "fame, glory, renown"; it is also in use as a surname.

Lazy Talk Word:
Rowemanse – a love affair; to have romance.
Proper Talk Word:
Romance – a fictitious tale of heroes and adventure; a sentimental novel dealing with love; to be passionate with your significant other or of anything.

(S)

Lazy Talk Word:
Saabith – the weekly day of rest, Sunday for most Christians and Saturday for Jews.
Proper Talk Word:
Sabbath - a day of religious observance and abstinence from work, kept by Jews from Friday evening to Saturday evening, and by most Christians on Sunday.

Lazy Talk Word:
Sabbowetaug – fake friend; someone to switch a good message into a bad message, or bad being.
Proper Talk Word:
Sabotage – Deliberate phonies; a person that talks about you behind your back in a bad way.

Lazy Talk Word:
Saycred – Holy; religious; worthy of respect.

Proper Talk Word:
Sacred - connected with God (or the gods) or dedicated to a religious purpose and so deserving veneration; (of writing or text) embodying the laws or doctrines of a religion.

Lazy Talk Word:
Sayphe – not dangerous; a box like metal container that is used to open with a key or combination for keeping valuable items or cash inside.

Proper Talk Word:
Safe – unhurt; (of writing or text) embodying the laws or doctrines of a religion; a strong fireproof cabinet with a complex lock, used for the storage of valuables.

Lazy Talk Word:
Saphfire – a blue colored candy diamond or birthstone.

Proper Talk Word:
Sapphire - a transparent precious stone, typically blue, that is a variety of corundum (aluminum oxide).

Lazy Talk Word:
Seene – a view; a subdivision of a movie or play showing one continuous action.

Proper Talk Word:
Scene – a view; a setting; a display of temper.

Lazy Talk Word:
Syeance – the study of natural phenomena or the knowledge so acquired.

Proper Talk Word:
Science – any branch of knowledge; an activity requiring study and method.

Lazy Talk Word:
Scripp – handwriting; the text of a film (movie), play, etc.

Proper Talk Word:
Script -handwriting as distinct from print; written characters; the written text of a play, movie, or broadcast.

Lazy Talk Word:
Scripta – a sacred writings in a Bible.

Proper Talk Word:
Scripture - the sacred writings of Christianity contained in the Bible.

Lazy Talk Word:
Scrowe – a rolled document with, two circled bars at each end of the scroll.

Proper Talk Word:
Scroll - a roll of parchment or paper for writing or painting on.

Lazy Talk Word:
Skopcher – the art of making statues or other shaped figures out of clay, glass, etc.

Proper Talk Word:
Sculpture - the art of making two or three dimensional representative or abstract forms, especially by carving stone or wood or by casting metal or plaster.

Lazy Talk Word:
Seeur's – to dry up, the store name (called Sears); to wither; to burn the surface of.

Proper Talk Word:
Sear - burn or scorch the surface of (something) with a sudden, intense heat; to cause withering or drying.

Lazy Talk Word:
Searies – a group of related things or movies, coming one after another; succession.

Proper Talk Word:
Series - a number of things, events, or people of a similar kind or related nature coming one after another.

Lazy Talk Word:
Cirius – to be sincere; sober.

Proper Talk Word:
Serious – (of a subject, state, or activity) demanding

careful consideration or application.

Lazy Talk Word:
Sirusly – you for real; you not joking; not opinionated.
Proper Talk Word:
Seriously – to be for real; to not joke at all; factual.

Lazy Talk Word:
Cex – either of two divisions of orgasms according to reproductive function, male and female; to have sex.
Proper Talk Word:
Sex – the urge or instinct to copulate; sexual intercourse; if someone is male or female.

Lazy Talk Word:
Shaph – a bar; along narrow passage.
Proper Talk Word:
Shaft – the body of a spear or arrow.

Lazy Talk Word:
Cylowet – a drawing consisting of an outline filled in with a solid color.
Proper Talk Word:
Silhouette - the dark shape and outline of someone or something visible against a lighter background, especially in dim light.

Lazy Talk Word:
Cylk – thread or fabric of lustrous fiber produced by an Asian caterpillar; silk worm; a name of a musical group.
Proper Talk Word:
Silk - a fine, strong, soft, lustrous fiber produced by silkworms in making cocoons and collected to make thread and fabric; a name of a music group.

Lazy Talk Word:
Cylva/Cilva – a white metallic element valued for jewelry, tableware, and coinage; a person's name; a color.

Proper Talk Word:
Silver/Sylva – coins of this metal; tableware of this metal; a lustruous grey; a precious shiny grayish-white metal, the chemical element of atomic number 47.

Lazy Talk Word:
Seng – to perform vocal music; a song being sung.
Proper Talk Word:
Sing – to utter words or sounds in musical tones.

Lazy Talk Word:
Cip – a small amount of liquid that anyone drinks.
Proper Talk Word:
Sip - a small mouthful of liquid.

Lazy Talk Word:
Cir – a respectful form of address to someone; someone's name; to have manners while in the military.
Proper Talk Word:
Sir - used as a polite or respectful way of addressing a man, especially one in a position of authority.

Lazy Talk Word:
Slaang – ghetto talk, ebonic's talk, lazy talk.
Proper Talk Word:
Slang - language peculiar to a particular group, such as: jardon.

Lazy Talk Word:
Sleaque – glossy; neat; to polish.
Proper Talk Word:
Sleek - (of hair, fur, or skin) smooth and glossy.
Lazy Talk Word:
Clique – smooth, sly, sneaky.
Proper Talk Word:
Slick – glossy and slippery; shrewd; superficially attractive but without substance.

Lazy Talk Word:
Snuppe - investigate or look around furtively in an attempt to find out something, especially

information about someone's private affairs.

Proper Talk Word:
Snoop - a furtive investigation; to pry; a lever; to look curiously or inquisitively.

Lazy Talk Word:
Soulstiss – either of 2 times of the year when the sun takes the most northerly or most southerly path across the sky.

Proper Talk Word:
Solstice – a part of someone's name; either of the two times in the year, the summer solstice and the winter solstice, when the sun reaches its highest or lowest point in the sky at noon, marked by the longest and shortest days.

Lazy Talk Word:
Sawnitt – a fourteen line poem divided into an octet and a sestet.

Proper Talk Word:
Sonnet - a poem of fourteen lines using any of a number of formal rhyme schemes, in English typically having ten syllables per line.

Lazy Talk Word:
Sowle – the essential, spiritual, or immortal part of a person; deep feelings; to care in-depth.

Proper Talk Word:
Soul - emotional or intellectual energy or intensity, especially as revealed in a work of art or an artistic performance.

Lazy Talk Word:
Spaid – a playing card marked with a black inverted heart; a name of a card game.

Proper Talk Word:
Spade - a black figure that resembles a stylized spearhead on each playing card of one of the four suits

Lazy Talk Word:
Spektackula – striking or showy; to be like a master in something.
Proper Talk Word:
Spectacular - beautiful in a dramatic and eye-catching way; an event such as a pageant or musical, produced on a large scale and with striking effects.

Lazy Talk Word:
Sporce – to play a game, such as: football, basketball, tennis, soccer, etc; a fun-loving person.
Proper Talk Word:
Sports – an active pastime or diversion, especially a game; light mockery; a loveable person that brings out the fun in a person; to display.

Lazy Talk Word:
Swagga – to strut, to brag; a person's name.
Proper Talk Word:
Swagger – to walk insolently; walk or behave in a very confident and typically arrogant or aggressive way.

Lazy Talk Word:
Cylvester – a silver garment that represents power; a person's name; a color; don't approve of a smart aleck.
Proper Talk Word:
Sylvester - a name derived from the Latin adjective silvestris meaning "wooded" or "wild", which derives from the noun silva meaning "woodland"; a dark cholate handsome thing, so sexy you can't live without; can get smart a lot, meaning to not be a smart aleck.

(T)

Lazy Talk Word:
Tallint – a natural ability or beauty; very smart and talented.
Proper Talk Word:
Talent – to have a natural aptitude or skill.

Lazy Talk Word:
Tanjareen – a orangelike fruit with easily peeled skin.
Proper Talk Word:
Tangerine - a small citrus fruit with a loose skin, especially one of a variety with deep orange-red skin.

Lazy Talk Word:
Tatts – a permanent ink mark on the skin that is in a specific design as requested by the individual with the tattoo.
Proper Talk Word:
Tattoo – a permanent mark made on the skin by pricking and with permanent ink.

Lazy Talk Word:
Tiniss – a game played with rackets and a light ball that is colored green on a court divided by a net.
Proper Talk Word:
Tennis - a game in which two or four players strike a ball with rackets over a net stretched across a court.

The usual form (originally called lawn tennis) is played with a felt-covered hollow rubber ball on a grass, clay, or artificial surface.

Lazy Talk Word:
Gat – to do something in a specific kind of way which causes you to ask – Like that (gat).
Proper Talk Word:
That – a person, thing, or idea indicated, mentioned, or understood from the situation.

Lazy Talk Word:
Top – above something or someone; the white house.
Proper Talk Word:
Top- to the highest or uppermost point, part, or surface of something.

Lazy Talk Word:
Traeverce – to travel across or through; a car and a person's name.

Proper Talk Word:
Traverse – lying across;
crosswise; a name of a car
and an individual's name.

Lazy Talk Word:
Traboot – a gift or act as
acknowledgment of respect;
a car name; a person's name.
Proper Talk Word:
Tribute – a name of a
cell phone and truck; a
payment, often forced,
from 1 nation to another
as acknowledgment of
submission.

Lazy Talk Word:
Tryumf – success.
Proper Talk Word:
Triumph – to rejoice over a
victory.

Lazy Talk Word:
Truss – confident belief;
to be true; part of a bank's
name.
Proper Talk Word:
Trust – firm reliance;
care; to depend or rely on
someone or something; a
name of a bank.

Lazy Talk Word:
Toon – to adjust for
maximum performance.
Proper Talk Word:
Tune – a simple
arrangement of pleasing
musical tones.

Lazy Talk Word:
Tuner – to make something
better; a nickname.
Proper Talk Word:
Turner – a person's name;
a skilled wood or lathe
turning.

(U)

Lazy Talk Word:
uKason – an authoritative
decree; a person's name.
Proper Talk Word:
uKase – a proclamation of
the czar having the force
of law in Russia; a person's
name.

Lazy Talk Word:
Unabetted – at original full
force.

Proper Talk Word:
Unabated - without any reduction in intensity or strength.

Lazy Talk Word:
Upliph – to raise to a higher social, intellectual or moral level.
Proper Talk Word:
Uplift - elevate or stimulate (someone) morally or spiritually.

Lazy Talk Word:
Uprite – honorable.
Proper Talk Word:
Upright – morally respectable.

(V)

Lazy Talk Word:
Vaykayshun – an interval of time devoted to rest or relaxation from work, study, etc; to take a vacation.
Proper Talk Word:
Vacation - an extended period of leisure and recreation, especially one spent away from home or in traveling.

Lazy Talk Word:
Vasallet – to change your mind often.
Proper Talk Word:
Vacillate – to oscillate; waver.

Lazy Talk Word:
Vantij – something provided for superiority or advantage.
Proper Talk Word:
Vantage - a place or position affording a good view of something.

Lazy Talk Word:
Varyittable – to be true.
Proper Talk Word:
Veritable – unquestionable trust.

Lazy Talk Word:
Vess – to place authority, power in the control of; a garment worn overtop a shirt.

Proper Talk Word:
Vest – to dress in an ecclesiastical garment; a sleeveless garment worn over a shirt.

Lazy Talk Word:
Vetarin – a person of long experience in an activity; a former member of the armed forces.

Proper Talk Word:
Veteran - a person who has had long experience in a particular field; a person who has served in the military.

(W)

Lazy Talk Word:
Waga – to bet; a person's name.

Proper Talk Word:
Wager – a person's name; more formal term for bet.

Lazy Talk Word:
Wagin – a 4 wheeled vehicle or toy with a large rectangular body.

Proper Talk Word:
Wagon - a vehicle used for transporting goods or another specified purpose.

Lazy Talk Word:
Websight – a set of interconnected webpages prepared as a collection of information, by a person or organization.

Proper Talk Word:
Website - a location connected to the Internet that maintains one or more pages on the World Wide Web.

Lazy Talk Word:
Wede – a medicinal plant used for to become highly medicated to fix glaucoma, depression, and other illnesses; marijuana plant; weed plant; an aquatic plant, such as: seaweed plant; a person's name.

Proper Talk Word:
Weed - a plant that is not valued where it is growing and is usually of vigorous

growth; legal medical marijuana; a person's name.

Lazy Talk Word:
Wellcum – permitted to do and likes it a lot; to accept gladly.
Proper Talk Word:
Welcome – received with hospitality; gratifying; to greet cordially.

Lazy Talk Word:
What's up – to keep track of different happenings.
Proper Talk Word:
What is up – to know what is happening at all times.

Lazy Talk Word:
What's Happening – to ask someone how they are doing; a figure of speech.
Proper Talk Word:
What is happening – to ask a question to know the what currently is happening.

Lazy Talk Word:
What's going on – to ask someone how they personal doing.

Proper Talk Word:
What is going on – a name of a song that is sung by Marvin Gaye.

Lazy Talk Word:
Whiting – a name of a tattoo; the color of snow; a race; a business name.
Proper Talk Word:
White – of the color of milk or fresh snow, due to the reflection of most wavelengths of visible light; the opposite of black.

Lazy Talk Word:
Whin – victory; supportive; a movie or a person's name.
Proper Talk Word:
Win – to achieve victory; to receive as a prize; to gain the support of.

Lazy Talk Word:
Whyne/Wein – the fermented juice of grapes or other fruits; a city call Schweinfurt in Germany.
Proper Talk Word:
Wine - the alcoholic usually fermented juice of a plant

product (such as a fruit) used as a beverage; a name of a city in Germany called Schweinfurt.

Lazy Talk Word:
Wonda – to be curious; to feel auh.
Proper Talk Word:
Wonder – a marvel; awe; doubtful.

(X)

Lazy Talk Word:
Zenofile – a person attracted to foreign culture and people; like foreign manner.
Proper Talk Word:
Xenophile - an individual who is attracted to foreign peoples, manners, or cultures.

(Y)

Lazy Talk Word:
Yott – a small sailing vessel, used for pleasure cruises or racing; a yacht boat.
Proper Talk Word:
Yacht - a medium-sized sailboat equipped for cruising or racing.

Lazy Talk Word:
Yuh – a saying; German word meaning yes; a person's name; a website name.
Proper Talk Word:
Ya - ("yes") with the emphatic wohl placed after it, meaning "it is willed"; another name for Ja; a website search engine name.

Lazy Talk Word:
Yauh – saying while having sex; to deviate from the intended course, as a ship.
Proper Talk Word:
Yaw - a twisting or oscillation of a moving ship or aircraft around a vertical axis.

Lazy Talk Word:
Yes Sir – To be polite; cool points comment; to have manners; military respect comment to Officers.

Proper Talk Word:
Yes Sir – to like what is being done or said; to have respect for a military officer.

conservation, or display to the public.

(Z)

Lazy Talk Word:
Zeebrauh – a black and white stripe horse-like African mammal.

Proper Talk Word:
Zebra - an African wild horse with black-and-white stripes and an erect mane.

Lazy Talk Word:
Zu – a park in which living animals are kept and exhibited.

Proper Talk Word:
Zoo - an establishment which maintains a collection of wild animals, typically in a park or gardens, for study,

PUNCTUATION MARKS FOR SOME WORDS

These punctuations are symbols for how to pronounce and/or use the word(s).

Apostrophe

1. To form the possessive case of action words, verbs, and names/places.
   - Example: The woman's scarf.
   - Example: To meet Wagners' dad.

2. To make it plural of single letters, figures, and symbols.
   - Example: Three r's; 2 by 4's, etc.

Brackets

3. In pairs, are used to indicate a word or phrase that is extraneous, incidental, or explanatory, within quoted material.
   - Example: The King [Justice] ordered him to leave. "I received [wealth] from your package.

4. In pairs, are used to set off parenthetical material within other parenthetical material.
   - Example: Act of February 29, 2004 (ch.3 sec. [or] 229).

Colon

5. Use this to introduce a series.
   - Example: Four items were purchased: a painting a statue, 2 book that is copyrighted, and then published.

Comma

6. Use this to separate independent clauses not joined by a conjuction when the clauses are short, closely related, and have no commas within.
   - Example: I can, I went, and I win.

7. Use this to separate two words or figures that might otherwise be misunderstood.
   - Example: To Amanti, James was nice.

8. Use this to set apart an explanatory, defining, or emphatic phrase.
   - Example: Foods – meats, fish, and eggs.

Dash

9. There are two kinds of dashes: the most common is the em dash, so called because it is roughly the same width as a capital M in the typeface being used. The en dash is half the length of the em dash but longer than the hyphen.
   - The em dash is used to indicate a sudden break or abrupt change in continuity: "If-if you'll just let me explain," the student stammered.
   - The em dash is used to set apart an explanatory, defining, or emphatic phrase:

Foods rich in protein – meat, fish, and eggs – should be eaten daily.

- The em dash is used to set apart parenthetical matter:
  Kareem, in spite of his achievements – and he had many – was a great Prince.
- The em dash is used to mark an unfinished sentence:
  "But if my bus is late – "he began.
- The em dash is used to set off a summarizing phrase or clause:
  Julian Barnes, and John Green – these are among America's most prominent prose writers of the 19ᵗʰ century.
- The em dash is used to set off the name of an author or source, as at the end of a quotation:
  A poet can survive everything but a misprint. – Oscar Wilde.
- The en dash is used to indicate or set apart numbers and words when the meaning is through, to, or from … to: The years 2000-2004 were politically divisive. Eva Peron (1919-52) was born to a poor family in Buenos Aires.
- The en dash is used to set apart the elements of a compound adjective when one of the elements consists of two words:
  the pre-Civil War era; a Pulitzer Prize – winning novel.

Ellipsis

10. There are two kinds of ellipsis.

- The ellipsis with three spaced points is used to indicate the omission of words or sentences within quotes matter:

  Equipped by education to rule in the nineteenth century...he lived and reigned in his country or origin in the twentieth century. – Robert, K.

- The ellipsis with four spaced points is used to indicate the omission of words at the end of a sentence:

  The timidity of bureaucrats when it comes to dealing with...triumph is easy to explain...- New York.

Exclamation Point

11. The exclamation point is used to mark surprise, incredulity, admiration, or other strong emotion:

  What! How beautiful! "Excellent!" he shouted. Who shouted, "All aboard!"

Hyphen

12. Use this to join the elements of some compounds.

- Example: Attorney-at-Law; great-grandma (paternal), and suitcases.

Parentheses

13. Parentheses are used to set off nonessential, supplementary, or explanatory material.

- Example: She bought two dresses for $16.00 in 1999, but $22.00 in 2019.
- Example: The result is only for original works, which provides your theory.
- Example: Ms. Perkins belongs to the Portland (Ore.) Chamber of Commerce.

14. Parentheses are used to enclose parenthetical material where the interruption is too great to be indicated by commas.
    - Example: You can find it neither in American catalogues (at any rate, not in Sears') nor will you find it in New Zealand magazines.

15. Parentheses are used to enclose letters or numbers in a series.
    - Example: The order of deliveries will be (a) mail, (b) groceries, and (c) laundry, if any.
    - Example: The cars are (1) old-fashioned, (2) still in good condition, and (3) quite expensive.

Period

16. Use this to mark the end of a sentence or sentence fragment that is neither exclamatory nor interrogatory.
    - Example: Stuffed fish and stuffed shrimp is delicious.

17. Use this to abbreviate.
    - Example: U.S.A.; Dr.

18. Use this before a decimal and between dollars and cents in figures.
    • Example: 45 euro's; 25.1 feet; $29.91.

Question Mark

19. The question mark is used to mark the end of a direct query, even if not in the form of a question.
    • Example: "Could she tell from the sweatpants?" he asked. Can there be a promotional raise? Is the question.

20. The question mark is used to express uncertainty or doubt.
    • Example: Pocahontas (1595?-1617), American German Princess; the mail clerk said the book weighed 50 (?) pounds.

Quotation Mark

21. Double quotation marks are used to enclose direct quotations.
    • Example: "Kia," asked Kathy, "why are you singing?"

22. Double quotation marks are used to enclose titles of speeches or lectures, articles, short poems, short stories, chapters of books, songs, short musical compositions, radio and TV programs.
    • Example: A lecture entitled "The Atomic Era" The article "The Gypsies" appeared in the last issue. She read Shirley Jackson's "The Lottery"

and Keat's "Ode on a Grecian Urn." The chorus sang "God Bless America." We watched "Nova" on PBS.

23. Double quotation marks are used to enclose coined words, slang expressions, or ordinary, words, etc., used ironically or in some other unusual way.
   • Example: references to the "imperial Presidency" of Richard Nixon; George Herman "Babe" Ruth; His report was "bunk".

Semicolon

24. The semicolon is used to separate clauses containing commas.
   • Example: Rachel Smith, president of the National Bank, was also a director of Acme Lumber Co.; Harvey Jones, chairman of the board of Williams & Sons, was also on the board of American Steel Co. No. sir; I do not recall.

25. The semicolon is used to separate independent clauses joined by conjunctive adverbs.
   • Example: The supervisor praised his work highly; therefore, he was given a raise.

26. The semicolon is used to separate statements that are too closely related to be written as separate sentences, and also contrasting statements.
   • Example: War is destructive; peace, constructive.

Virgule

27. Use this to substitute for the word or between the words and & or.
    - Example: I love my son and/or the same as he unconditionally loves me too.

www.ingramcontent.com/pod-product-compliance
Lightning Source LLC
Chambersburg PA
CBHW050401290526
45786CB00003B/1075